That Special Someone
(A Jewish Romance Novel)

First Edition.

ISBN: 978-1512015539

That Special Someone

By

Chaya T. Hirsch

Also by Chaya T. Hirsch:

Meant To Be

Shira's Secret

Aviva's Pain

Malky's Heart

Losing Leah

Dear reader,

For your convenience, a Hebrew/Yiddish glossary of Jewish phrases and terms is available after the last chapter of this book.

Chapter One

It's official. I'm the worst employee in the world.

Okay, it's my first day and I shouldn't be too hard on myself, but who breaks the copy machine after only five minutes?

I stand awkwardly on the side while my boss, Mr. Markus, inspects different parts of the machine, hoping and praying he can find a solution to the problem. Because if not, he'll have to call a guy to come check it out. That may take days. And the tax due date for many clients is tomorrow. Working without the copy machine—which is also a fax and a printer—would be like living without a liver. At least that's what Mr. Markus said.

He's on his knees and glances at me with a wry smile. "Maybe I should have hired the other girl."

My face heats up. My coworkers try to hide their laughs.

Mr. Markus's dark brown eyes light up as he chuckles. "I'm kidding. Don't beat yourself up over it, Adina. First days are never easy."

A small smile crawls onto my face as a bit of relief washes over me. He doesn't hate me. Well, at least now the whole office knows I'm clumsy. I'm glad the secret is out.

Mr. Markus closes the latch and gets up. His black yarmulke almost slides off his head, but he catches it in time. He's really tall, and I need to raise my head to look at him since I'm barely five-two. "I'll ask Yehoshua to look at it when he gets in," he says. "If he can't fix it, I'll just have to call the company."

"I'm, um. I'm sorry," I stammer, my fingers getting tangled in my frizzy, black hair. I can feel the eyes of the other girls on me, still enjoying the show. My first impression sucks. It's just a fact of my life.

Mr. Markus grins. "It's okay. For now, can you do some filing?"

I nod. Filing is good. The worst that can happen is that I'll get a paper cut or that my finger will get caught in a drawer.

"Thanks," he calls over his shoulder as he enters his office and closes the door behind him.

That Special Someone

I'm left standing in the corner of the room with five pairs of eyes blinking at me.

I laugh lamely. "Hi. I'm Adina Reid." My wave is equally lame.

None of them says anything. Then a girl who looks around my age with a dirty blonde wig—I notice she's the only one here who's married—waves. "I'm Miriam Lowenger." She starts to introduce the other girls, but she says the names so fast they zoom right past my ears. I saw a couple of them last week at my interview, but I haven't had the chance to meet them yet because I arrived extremely early this morning. Mr. Markus asked me to make copies. And, well, the rest is history.

"Thanks for breaking the machine," a girl with short, light brown hair says, a twinkle in her eye. "Now I don't have to work on Gerwitz's tax return." She leans back in her chair and stretches her arms. "His documents are a mess."

"Has this, um…has this ever happened before?" I ask. "The machine breaking?"

All five of them giggle. "No. Mr. Markus just bought it a few weeks ago," Miriam says.

I groan. "I should win an award."

They laugh again.

The rest of them seem to be a few years younger than my twenty-five years. They're still smiling. I'm glad they're making me feel better about the whole copy machine fiasco.

Miriam gets up from her chair and points to a medium-sized bin on the floor. Files are piled up inside. "You can start with those. Then you can file these." She nods to a stack of papers on her desk. She smiles apologetically. "Sorry."

"It's okay. I won't break the file cabinet. At least, I hope so."

My coworkers laugh again.

After pushing my glasses higher up on my nose, I gather a few files in my arms and walk into a semi-large room with a round table and chairs—I guess this is the conference room. The files are behind the table. Miriam comes over and gives me a quick explanation of the cabinets, and then I'm on my own. After what happened this morning, I'm glad to be alone to wallow in self-pity. This sort of thing always happens to me. I'm not sure if it's because I'm a natural klutz, or because it's just one of those things. Bad luck or whatever.

About an hour later, the front door to the office opens and I hear someone walk in. From where I am in the room, I can't see the person, but I hear a masculine voice. Then I hear Mr.

That Special Someone

Markus. The words "copy machine" and "broken" are exchanged, and it takes every bit of me not to scold myself for doing something so silly.

I'm on my knees at the bottom drawer when Mr. Markus's head pops into the room. "Adina, can you come here, please?"

I place the files on the table before following him to the copy machine. There is a guy crouched by it, peering inside. After a few seconds, he closes the latch and stands. I realize he looks just like Mr. Markus. He has the same dark brown hair and eyes and the same slim build. He is a good few inches taller than him. This must be Mr. Markus's son—he told me he works here. When he sees me standing before him, he says, "Ah, so this is the girl who vandalized my father's property."

I know he's kidding because he has nothing but humor in his eyes. Because he's so tall, it's almost like I'm staring at the ceiling. "Um…it just happened," I mumble.

He opens another latch. "Like I told my father, it takes a lot of talent to break the machine on your first day." He looks at me and grins. "Talent like that is good. You'll be a great asset to the team."

I'm not sure if he's teasing or complimenting me. Maybe both. I feel my entire face and neck heat up. The guy is very

5

good-looking. I think he's my age, maybe a little older. And when I scan the room, I see some of the other girls looking at him and whispering to one another.

I wonder if he's single.

Wait, what? I quickly shake my head.

"I'm sorry?" he asks.

Did I say something? I know I sometimes mutter to myself when I tell my mind to shut up. "I'm Adina Reid," I blurt, my cheeks still warm.

"Yehoshua Markus." He crouches by the machine again. "Do you know what you did?"

"Not really. The machine ran out of paper, so I put some in."

"Hmm…" He opens another latch. "Ah, here's the problem. The machine tried to print on the wrong paper. It got jammed in here." He stretches his hand inside and pulls out a crumpled piece of paper.

"Oh." I laugh sheepishly. "The machine at my last job wasn't like that." Wow, can I sound any more lame?

Yehoshua presses a button and the machine starts to work again. "No problem." He glances at his dad. "I think it's fine."

Mr. Markus claps him on the back. "And to think I would

have paid a few hundred dollars to some tech guy."

"You can give that money to me," he jokes.

Mr. Markus rubs the back of his head before giving him a slight shove. "Get out of here."

Before he disappears from my view, I study his left hand. No ring. It's common for some Orthodox Jewish men to not wear wedding bands, so I have no idea if he's married. But by judging by how the other girls are still whispering and giggling, it's safe to say he's not.

I quickly shake my head again. Seriously.

We all return to work. I'm once again glad to be alone filing, though I wish my mind would keep quiet. It's not the end of the world that I made a fool of myself in front of a guy. It wouldn't be the first time. At least I don't have to worry about Yehoshua Markus rejecting me for accidentally spilling coffee on his pants.

At twelve o'clock, my boss tells me I have an hour for lunch break. I figure I might as well take it now. I return to my desk and rummage in my bag for the sandwich I made. Peanut butter and jelly. I know, I'm not five years old, but I love it.

"Hey," Miriam says from the desk next to me. "Some of us are eating in the conference room. You're welcome to join us."

"Okay. Thanks."

Crowds make me nervous. I guess I'm not the most social person out there. But I don't want to ice myself out, especially not on the first day. I gather my sandwich and drink and sit down near the girl with the light brown hair, the one who was very appreciative about my breaking the machine.

The conversation seems to revolve around someone's engagement. It's not a topic I like to discuss, since I'm twenty-five and every single one of my friends, other than Avigayil, are married and have been for quite a few years. I've never made it past a second date. Most of the girls here seem to be in their early twenties, so I guess they're not burned out yet.

As I sip my drink, I realize they're not talking about a random girl but Mr. Markus's daughter.

"Oh," I say, "I didn't know Mr. Markus's daughter is engaged." Not that I would, since I don't know the family. I guess I felt like I had to say something instead of sitting here as though I'm another chair at the table.

"She's getting married next week," Light-Brown-Haired Girl says.

"Oh cool."

They smile.

That Special Someone

"Can you tell me your names again?" I ask. "I'm Adina."

"Michal," Light Brown Hair says. The others introduce themselves as Faigy, Shaindy, and Naomi.

"Does anyone else work here?" I ask.

"Just Mr. Markus and his son," Miriam says.

Two of the girls—Michal and Naomi—sort of giggle at the mention of Yehoshua.

"He's um…" I clear my throat. "Handy with the copy machine."

They're giving me weird looks.

"Is he married?" I blurt, then kick myself.

"Nope," Naomi says, her face a little bright. Maybe out of hope?

"He's…difficult," Miriam says. Then she shakes her head. "Maybe we shouldn't talk about this."

"Difficult how?" I ask. Then I take a large bite of my sandwich so I'll keep quiet.

"The girl who worked here before you," Miriam says. "She and Yehoshua dated. It didn't end well. That's why she quit."

"Oh."

"We don't know what happened," Faigy says. "Suri just quit without an explanation, so we assume it was because of

Yehoshua."

"*Assuming* he was the one who hurt her," Naomi says. "It's possible *she* was the one who hurt *him*."

Michal rolls her eyes. "He's not going to go out with you, Naomi. The matchmaker said he thought it wasn't a match."

She frowns, though I still see hope in her eyes.

It doesn't feel right talking about him behind his back, so I change the subject. "How old are all of you?"

"Twenty-five," Miriam says.

"Cool. Me, too."

"Really? You look much younger."

I wave my hand. "Thanks. I get that a lot."

"Faigy is twenty-two," Michal says. "Shaindy is twenty, and Naomi and I are twenty-one. Is that a peanut butter and jelly sandwich?" She looks semi-disgusted and semi-appalled.

I wipe my mouth with the napkin I packed with my sandwich. "Yeah. Um, you all have accounting degrees or are studying accounting in school?"

They nod.

"Cool. I have an accounting degree, too."

"Mr. Markus only hires people with accounting backgrounds," Faigy says, like it's the most obvious thing in the world.

"Oh, that makes sense..."

"You'll like it here," Miriam says. "Mr. Markus is super lenient with many things, though you better not come late to work. He hates that."

"And if he's ever upset with you, just bring cookies or cake," Shaindy says. "He loves that."

"Thanks for the tips."

The room gets quiet.

After a few moments, Faigy starts talking about her friend who just had a baby. I stay here for a few minutes before throwing out my garbage and sitting down at my desk to browse online.

Hopefully soon, I won't feel like the new girl anymore.

Chapter Two

When the bus reaches my stop, I get off and walk the short five blocks to my house. Mom is working on supper. "Hey," I say, dropping my bag on the table and falling into a chair.

"Hey, sweetie. How was your first day?"

"It was…fine." If you don't count the part where I jammed the copy machine. "The boss seems nice and my coworkers are very kind and welcoming." Even though I felt a little out of place when I talked to them.

She smiles. "I'm glad. I hope you like it more than your last job."

Mom is a little upset that I quit my last job. The pay was good—much better than what I'll make at Markus Accounting, though in my defense, I am starting from the bottom—but I worked there for five years and needed a change of scenery.

That Special Someone

The truth is, I loved my last job. But everyone was moving on, getting married, having kids. And I was still there, remaining the same.

She wipes her hand on a dish towel before sitting down near me. "Listen, Adina. The matchmaker called. She needs an answer."

I puff out some air and stare at the ceiling. I've been pushing this off because I don't want to deal with it. Another guy. Another rejection. A little piece of my heart breaking off. Okay, maybe the last part is a bit extreme, but rejection *hurts*. Not moving past a second date *hurts*. I don't want to think about this. I wish I could just go up to my room and continue working on the game I'm designing.

Mom rubs my hand. "He sounds like a good guy from a really good family. Why are you so hesitant?"

I sigh. "He'll say no. Like the others."

"You don't know that."

"How many guys have I been out with in the five years I've been dating?"

"Adina."

"How many?"

Now she sighs. "Over forty."

"And how many of them liked me?"

"*Adina.*"

I stand and reach for my bag. "Just tell her whatever you want. I'm so sick of this. I'm going to my room."

When I'm at the foot of the stairs, Mom says, "One day, with God's help, you'll meet the right one. And then you'll realize that all this was worth it."

I bite my lower lip as tears threaten to enter my eyes. I have an older sister and three older brothers and every one of them got married within two years of dating. Mom has never held that over my head. She doesn't like to compare us. But why am I having such a hard time? I just don't get it.

Maybe I am a weirdo.

Just as I enter my room, my phone beeps. It's a text from my best friend, Avigayil, asking me to come over because she has some news to share. She wasn't always my best friend or even a good friend. We had a large group of friends in high school and would always hang out. Then after high school, our mutual friends would invite us to get together, and we were friendly, just never *good* friends. As the years went on, more and more of our group started to get engaged and then married. While we all tried to keep in touch, things changed. Slowly,

That Special Someone

Avigayil and I grew closer and now we are the only two single girls left in our group. We've become best friends.

I tell my mom where I'm going and head to the driveway. We only have one car and Mom uses it for work while I take the bus. I get in and start the engine, peeling away from the curb. Avigayil lives fifteen minutes away. I park in her driveway and ring the bell. After she welcomes me inside and I say hello to her family, we sit on the porch in front of her house with cans of Coke and pretzels. It's October here in Brooklyn, New York, so it's a little chilly outside. But it's the only place we have privacy.

Avigayil munches on a pretzel, the wind blowing her medium brown hair into her eyes. "So how was work?"

"I broke the copy machine."

"What?"

I can't help but laugh. It hasn't been that long ago, but it feels like it. I'm ready to look back on it with only fond memories. "Well, I jammed it. My boss's son fixed it."

"Why am I not surprised?" she says with a smile.

"Classic Adina, right?"

"Ten points."

I sit back on the chair and gulp down some Coke. "There

are five other girls working there. Now I have no choice but to be social." I only had two coworkers at my last job because it was a small office. It didn't take me too long to warm up to them. But five coworkers is a whole different story. Well, there technically are six coworkers if I include Yehoshua Markus, but I don't have to worry about having anything but a professional relationship with him. As Orthodox Jews, we don't really mingle with the opposite gender.

"You're fine, Adina," Avigayil assures me. "Don't get caught up in that."

"But I'm so awkward around people, especially ones I just meet."

I think back to the last guy I went out with. Eli…whatever his last name was. I mentally roll my eyes. Who am I kidding? Of course I know his last name. It's Schwartz. I liked him, but apparently he didn't share my feelings. A part of me thinks it had to do with the fact that I accidentally dragged mud into his brand new car. Or maybe it was because I accidentally wore a shirt that had a large stain. Mom wasn't home that night and I was a nervous wreck and didn't check myself properly. Ugh, I'm really a loser.

"It's just the way you are." Avigayil rubs my arm. "One day, you'll meet someone who loves that about you."

"If people would just get to know me..." They'd realize I'm actually fun and kind and loyal.

"They will."

"You know you didn't like me at first."

She hesitates. "Adina, let's not do this again. Please."

"I need to. I need to fix myself. If I'm such a ridiculous person—"

"You're not. You don't need to fix anything. For the record, I always thought you were cool. I just wanted to be like everyone else and fit in. But it's cool to be different. To be your own person."

"Not if it won't get me a third date."

She's quiet. When I glance at her, I see a frown on her face. I want to slap myself. Why do I always have to self-pity myself like this? Lately, all I've been doing when I hang out with Avigayil is whine. If I keep this up, I'll push her away, too.

"I'm sorry," I say. "You said you have news?"

She keeps her eyes on the spot in front of her for a bit before turning to me. "I'll feel like a jerk telling you this."

"Why? Oh, does it have to do with Shmuli Lerer?"

She's fighting a grin.

Chaya T. Hirsch

"Oh my gosh, it does!" I grab her arm. "*Tell me*."

The largest grin I've ever seen leaps onto her face. "We went out again last night. He's so amazing. I think things are getting very serious between us. He might be the one."

At first, my grin is probably just as wide as hers. I'm *so* happy for her, and I tell her that. But then negative thoughts start to crowd my mind. Lately, it's always been Avigayil and me. The only ones not married, sharing the woes of dating, being in the same stage for the past five years. If she were to get married, I'd be alone. I'm not great at making friends. Of course I want her to meet the right guy and live happily ever after, but at the same time, I know it will hurt me. Because it'll mean that she found her soulmate while mine is still floating out there somewhere. Assuming I even have one. Knowing my luck, someone else probably stole him.

Not wanting to show anything but pure happiness, I wrap my arms around her and hug her close. We've grown so close these past few years and she's been there for me. I don't know what I'd do without her. But I guess I'll need to let her go.

Chapter Three

Today is my second day of work. Let's hope I don't flood the toilet or cause a fire.

When I enter the office, Naomi is hanging up her jacket. She's the only one here, other than Mr. Markus, who is in his office. "Good morning," I greet her.

She returns it. Did she just force a smile? I'm probably just being paranoid and am imagining it.

I peek into my boss's office. "Good morning, Mr. Markus."

He looks up from the papers on his desk and grins. "What a treat. None of the other girls bother to wish me a good morning anymore. Good morning, Adina."

I smile, then walk out of his office and come face to face with Naomi. "You don't have to wish him a good morning, you know. He comes out a few minutes after we arrive and wishes us all a good morning."

"Oh." Did I just make my coworkers look bad? "So that's a thing?" I ask.

"Yeah. It's a way for him to make sure everyone's here on time."

She's looking at me like I committed the greatest sin in the world. "Thanks for telling me," I say.

She heads to her desk.

I don't think she likes me. No, I won't think like that. It takes some time for me to warm up to people. I need to remember that. I worked at the same place for five years and had gotten used to the people there. In time, I know I will get friendly with everyone here.

The files are calling my name. I walk over to the bin and get to work. I originally thought I had to file the large folders and then the papers on Miriam's desk, but I didn't realize how many loose papers were under the folders. Filing them all will take me years.

One by one, the rest of the girls start to arrive. They all wish me a good morning. And like Naomi said, a few minutes later my boss comes in and wishes them all a good morning.

About an hour later, my stack of papers doesn't seem to be

any smaller. I fight back a groan.

Miriam walks inside, gives me a sweet smile, and heads to one of the drawers. She pulls it open and leafs through the files. When she has the one she needs, she closes the drawer with her hip. "How's it going?" she asks.

"Good. Only one paper cut."

She smiles again. "Did anyone give you a tour of the office?"

"Mr. Markus sort of did yesterday."

"Okay. I just wanted to make sure. And you know you're welcome to take whatever you want from the kitchen. Though, it may be wise to leave the cakes and cookies for Mr. Markus."

We both chuckle.

"And make sure you drink lots and lots of water from the water cooler. Sorry, my husband is a nutritionist."

"Water is good. It's vital to our existence."

She nods. "See you later."

I return to my filing. A few seconds later, my throat is parched. Great, did Miriam *have* to tell me to drink water? Now I can't get anything out of my head but how amazing it would feel to have some cool liquid sliding down my throat.

Abandoning the papers on the table, I head to the kitchen

and pour myself a cup of water from the cooler. I wonder what goodies they have in here. I check the cabinets. Some crackers and cookies. Delicious-looking cookies. I reach for the box and study its contents. I'm sure Mr. Markus won't be too upset if one was missing. I bite into it. This is the most amazing cookie I have ever eaten in my life. I take another to eat during my break.

I swallow a few times. Once again, my throat is dry. I open the refrigerator and notice grape soda. I don't remember the last time I had that. I grab a cup and pour, then drink it in one gulp. It reminds me of my childhood. I pour myself another cup to drink later.

I turn around to head back to my filing, and I crash into something hard.

I hear a groan. Yehoshua Markus stands before me.

I stumble back. "I'm so sorry!" I say, then realize I can't see well.

"It's okay. Here, I caught them before they fell to the floor."

"My glasses. Thanks." As soon as I put them on, I notice a large purple stain on his dark blue shirt. "Your shirt! I'm so sorry. I—"

He looks down at himself, then at me, and flashes a grin. "Don't worry about it. I never really liked this shirt, anyway."

He disappears into the men's bathroom.

Oh. My. Gosh. I just spilled grape soda on my boss's son. Can I be an even bigger klutz? I'm so mortified I want to disappear forever.

Faigy walks into the kitchen. "Is everything okay here?" She glances at the floor.

I follow her gaze and notice some of the soda has spilled there. "Yeah," I say. "I just spilled something. I'll clean it up."

She grabs some paper towels from the women's bathroom and is about to bend down to clean the mess, but I tell her I'll do it. I want to clean this up as fast as possible and hide in the conference room so I don't cross paths with Yehoshua Markus for the rest of the day. Or for the rest of my life. Yeah, that seems like a better option.

"Really, I'm fine," I assure her.

"Okay." She leaves.

I clean the mess as fast as possible, praying he doesn't come out of the bathroom. When I'm done, I realize the floor is still sticky, but I'm not sure I can do anything about that. Mr. Markus told me yesterday that a woman comes to clean the office once a week, so I'm sure it's fine if it remains sticky until she does. Thinking it's best I don't attempt to pour myself another cup of grape soda, I return to the conference room with my half-smashed cookie and fall down on my knees in front of the bottom drawer.

I can't let this bother me. This is who I am. I can either accept it and live happily ever after, or I can moan about it for the rest of my life.

I just hope I one day meet a guy who won't mind getting sucked into my embarrassing episodes.

Lunchtime arrives faster than I expect. Like yesterday, the girls sit at the conference room table to eat. I join them. The topic of today once again revolves around weddings and babies, which is typical in my world since that's one of the most important things in life. I try to participate, but it's hard to break the wall. I don't know how long they've worked here, but they seem to be a tight group. It kind of feels like the first few days of ninth grade, when I tried to break into groups.

After I finish my sandwich—peanut butter and jelly again—I reach into my bag for my phone. I finished programming the first level of the game I'm designing last night, but I haven't had the chance to try it yet. When I find a mistake or something I don't like, I write it down in my special small notebook.

"What game is that?" Miriam cranes her neck to look at my phone. "Hey, that looks cool. Is it available on the iPhone?"

"Oh, it's not available anywhere." Yet. At least, I hope it's a yet. I haven't actually completed a good enough game to sell yet.

Her eyebrows crinkle.

"I made it," I explain. "And it's not done yet. I don't know if it will ever be done. I don't have as much time to work on it as I did in the past."

She blinks at me. The rest of the girls give me blank faces.

"Wait. You're saying you're making a game?" Faigy asks.

I nod.

"That's...interesting," Michal mumbles.

"What for?" Naomi asks, her nostrils flared.

"Um." I tuck some of my frizzy hair behind my ear. "It's fun?"

"Playing games is a waste of time," Naomi says, tossing her blonde hair behind her shoulder. "Why would you waste time making them?"

Ouch. Stab my heart. Doesn't she understand that this

project is my baby?

"My husband loves mobile games," Miriam says, giving me a smile. Then she frowns. "It would be nice if he would stop playing them and help more around the house, though."

Naomi raises her chin.

"Well, it's fun for me," I say, feeling like I need to defend my baby, though it doesn't seem like anyone cares. "And it's something I enjoy doing. So it's *not* a waste of time."

Naomi rolls her eyes and stabs her fork into her lettuce.

The room is engulfed in an awkward silence.

"I guess I'll get back to filing," I mutter.

As I'm bent over the files, I try not to let Naomi's words bother me. It's not the first time someone told me that designing mobile games is a waste of time. Many guys I went out with turned up their noses, especially when I told them how much I'd love to do it full time. Mom is supportive, but she hasn't always been. When I was in twelfth grade and told her it was my dream to be a game designer, she didn't like the idea at all. We argued about it, but eventually, I realized she was right. The best thing to do was get a degree and have a career and do my designing on the side. Considering she raised me alone since I was ten because my father walked out on us, she knows how hard it is to make a living. I don't want to cause her any more heartache.

The girls eventually return to work and I'm once again left alone. Thankfully, I haven't seen Yehoshua since the incident and I hope to keep it like that for the rest of my life. I know how impossible that is because there's no way I can avoid him forever, but I can hope.

At 3:00, Shaindy peeks her head into the room. "Mr. Markus wants to see you."

Oh no. Does he know I soiled his son's shirt? Maybe he wants me to pay for the cleaning bill.

I shake my head, telling myself to be reasonable. "Thanks, Shaindy."

I file the last document before taking a deep breath and heading to my boss's office. As soon as he sees me, he smiles. Okay, that's a good sign. Maybe I'm not in trouble. "Adina, please sit down."

I do.

"I'm trying to think of something to give you to work on. We don't want you filing for the rest of your life." He locks his fingers together, studying me. "You said you did corporate tax returns at your last job?"

"Yeah, mostly."

He picks up the phone and presses a number. "Yehoshua, please come see me."

My entire body grows rigid. Why, why, why? Doesn't he understand that I don't want to be within ten feet of his son?

Yehoshua sticks his head in. "Yeah, Dad?"

Mr. Markus motions for him to come in. "Please sit down."

Yehoshua lowers himself next to me. He gives me a quick nod. I avert my gaze to anywhere but in his direction.

"What are you—" He stops talking and stares at his son's shirt. "What happened?"

Can the floor please open up and swallow me?

Yehoshua glances at me with a small grin. "It's the result of an unfortunate accident."

Mr. Markus's eyebrows come together. "I hope your mother can get the stain out. It looks like an expensive shirt."

Earth to ground? Please swallow me up.

Yehoshua glances at me again, another small grin on his face. "It's okay, Dad. I never really liked the shirt, anyway."

I look at Yehoshua. That was…sweet of him. Clearly the shirt was expensive and I doubt he doesn't like it because he wore a similar one yesterday. And it appears as though he tried to get the stain out. But he didn't want to embarrass or insult me. That's very kind. He's very kind. None of the guys I've dated were kind when I wrecked their clothes.

No, I won't think about that. Anyway, Miriam told me yesterday that Yehoshua is difficult. I don't do well with difficult.

"What are you currently working on?" my boss asks his son.

"Gross's Kosher Bakery and Yitzy's Plumbing."

"When are their due dates?"

"Next week."

He looks at me, then back at his son. "All the other girls are booked for the next few weeks. I want Adina to start off with corporate tax returns, since she did that at her last job. Most of the companies are handled by you, Shaindy and Faigy, and they told me they currently don't need help." He taps his pen on his desk. "Are you okay with working on a new client?"

Yehoshua inclines his head.

"It's a bit tough, which is why I think Adina would be great help. The client owns many small companies. A lot of them have due dates coming up. Do you think you can handle it?"

"I'm sure I can, Dad."

"Okay, good. Start on him as soon as you finish your other work and tell Adina what you'd like her to do. You can continue filing in the meantime, Adina, and when you're done, ask one of the girls to show you how to use the program so you can start working on bank statements."

"Okay," I say, my body still frozen, though my mind is swamped with thoughts. He wants me to work with Yehoshua, the guy I spilled grape soda on. The same guy who makes it seem like he's okay with it. I don't feel so silly anymore.

Does he think I'm funny?

I shake my head again. I need to stop thinking that.

"Did you say something?" Mr. Markus asks. He and his son are staring at me with raised eyebrows.

Great, I mumbled to myself again. "No. I'm cool. I mean, I'm okay."

Mr. Markus nods. "Okay, you two are dismissed."

Both Yehoshua and I stand at the same time and turn toward each other, aiming to push our chairs aside to leave. He motions for me to go first, and I give him a thankful smile before marching out.

It seems as though I will no longer have to do the little job and will start actual work. That makes me really excited. But it

That Special Someone

makes me even more excited that I'm going to work with Yehoshua. But why? Is it because of the way he brushed off my mishap like it was no big deal? That makes my heart feel a bit warm. No guy I've met has made me feel okay with being me. When I first started dating, I tried to be different, more like other girls. But that never worked out. Not only did I come off as fake, but I wasn't happy. Now I'm one hundred percent myself, but that doesn't seem to make guys like me, either. I guess they're looking for someone different.

Is Yehoshua looking for someone different?

***

Mom practically knocks me down as soon as I open the door. "The Friedlanders said yes!"

"What?" I ask absentmindedly.

I've been consumed with my thoughts as soon as I left the bus. Thoughts about Yehoshua. Please, as if he'd like a girl like me. He seems so put together and poised and charismatic. I can't imagine him standing next to a clumsy girl like me. He was just nice to me because he's a nice person. That's it.

"Adina?"

"Hmm?"

"Is tomorrow evening okay? 6:00?"

31

"For what?"

Mom sighs. "Adina, you need to pull your head out of the clouds. Yossi Friedlander wants to go out with you. Is 6:00 tomorrow a good time?"

"He actually wants to go out with me? He hasn't heard from his other friends that I'm a hurricane?"

Mom purses her lips. "Adina."

"What? The last three boys I dated went to the same yeshiva as him and are the same age. Guys talk, you know."

She sighs again. "What am I going to do with you?"

I feel nothing but guilt as I see how hunched my mom's shoulders are. I don't mean to be a pain. I just don't want to get rejected again. Hurt again. "I'm sorry, Mom," I say. "6:00 is perfect."

Her face washes with relief. "I'll call Mrs. Shain. Go pick out an outfit. You know you can never make up your mind until five minutes before the boy arrives."

"Okay."

Chapter Four

Well, I'm all prettied up.

Makeup, contacts instead of glasses, my hair straightened instead of frizzy waves. I look at my reflection in the mirror. I look okay. I know I'm not the prettiest girl out there, but I'm cute and like the way I look. I just hope my nerves don't get the better of me and make me do something foolish.

No matter how many times I go out, my knees never stop shaking and my palms are sweaty. I wipe them on my skirt, but that doesn't help. Even though I don't feel overly excited about this date because I'm pretty sure he'll reject me like his friends did, it would be nice if he's the one. Then I can stop worrying whether I'll ever meet the right guy or spend the rest of my life alone.

I say a small prayer to God, asking Him to provide me with

His guidance and to help me not make a mess of myself in front of Yossi Friedlander.

Mom walks into the room to inspect me. I do a small spin. "Do I meet her majesty's expectations?" I do a small curtsy.

Mom shakes her head, laughing to herself. "Oh, Adina. You kill me." She studies my face, then my outfit. "Where's your jewelry?"

My hands fly to my ears. Then to my upper chest. I am sans gold. "Oh, I forgot." I head over to my dresser and open my jewelry box.

"My daughter is the only girl in the world who has a box full of jewelry but forgets to wear them."

I laugh lightly.

"I'm already feeling sorry for your husband. The poor man will lavish you with jewelry and you won't wear a single one."

"It would mean more to me if he'd play my game and love it."

Mom takes the necklace and fastens it around my neck. "Tonight, try to be more…"

"Normal?" I ask.

She shuts her eyes for a second. "I didn't mean it like that."

"It's okay. I know I suck as a daughter."

That Special Someone

She puts her hands on my shoulders and turns me around. "Don't ever say that."

"But Henny, Ruvi, Zevy, and Naftali have brought you nothing but *nachas*. Joy and pride. While I…"

She plays with my hair. "You're unique, Adina. But guys don't need to see that on the first date. Or the second one."

I look away from her. "Pretending to be someone I'm not will only ruin things."

"I don't want you to pretend to be anyone you're not. But you don't need to show off all your colors in the first hour. Let him get to know you slowly."

I don't say anything. I don't even know what to say. She's right, but she's also wrong. I know guys might be put off by me, but there's hope in me that one day I'll meet someone who won't be. Someone who will find me interesting.

The doorbell rings. I tense up.

Mom squeezes my shoulders before heading downstairs to welcome my knight in shining armor into the castle. She will bring him into the living room that has a tray sitting on the table, filled with baked goods and a drink. Yossi Friedlander will be munching on one of Mom's awesome cookies when I, the princess, will descend the stairs. We will lock eyes for a few seconds before we both look away, embarrassed. Then my mom will entrust me into the hands of a stranger.

Yeah, I've done this before.

I pace around in my room for a few minutes, trying to calm my nerves, and breathe. When I think enough time has passed, I go downstairs. The guy has glasses and dark blond hair with a black yarmulke on his head. He's wearing a suit, just like all the other guys do. As soon as I walk in, he jumps to his feet and gives me a smile, his cheeks flushed. I return the smile and feel my own face warm up.

"Enjoy your time," my mom says, opening the door for us. She gives me a wide smile, and I see the hope shining in her eyes. She wants to see me married so she can stop worrying about me.

The guy and I walk out to his car that's parked in the driveway. He opens the door for me, and I climb in, thanking him. Then he settles in and starts the engine.

He tells me what hotel lounge he wants to take me to. "I hope that's okay."

"It is," I tell him, even though I've been there countless times. It's one of those places all couples go to on first dates. But I don't hold it against him. If I was the guy, I would have no idea where to go.

He clutches the steering wheel tightly as he drives. I guess he's just as nervous as I am. The awkward silence doesn't help.

After a few minutes, he clears his throat. "So…um. You're an accountant?"

"Yep."

He waits for me to elaborate.

"Oh. Um, yeah, I just started working at my new job this week."

"Do you like it?"

"Yeah. I mean, I've only been filing these past few days, but the people there are nice and I feel welcomed."

He nods. "That's good."

"What about you?"

"Law school."

Right. I knew that. It was on the profile Mrs. Shain sent us. "Law school is cool," I say.

"It's hard."

"Yeah," I quickly say. "I didn't mean cool like it's no big deal. I just meant it's a cool profession. You know, like awesome."

He glances at me for a second before focusing on the road.

I want to bang my head against the window. I need to be normal. No nerves, no nerdy things coming out of my mouth. Normal.

"So…you have three brothers?" I ask.

He nods and starts telling me about them. Two are married and learn the Talmud full time while the third is single and a doctor. I stop myself before I say something silly, like how handy it is to have a doctor in the family, in case there's God forbid an emergency.

I don't think being silent works, though. But at least he's not looking at me like I'm weird anymore.

We reach the hotel and park in the lot. We enter the lounge and sit at one of the tables. We just look at each other.

"What are your hobbies?" he asks.

I'm about to start gushing about my programming, but I stop myself. There's nothing wrong with it, but it doesn't seem like something guys are interested in talking about. It's odd, because many of them like playing games, but they would rather not discuss the actual design and coding. Whatever, I guess. I stick with my other hobbies. "Reading, cooking. I like watching the water."

"Watching the water?"

"Yeah. Like, just staring at the waves. It's peaceful. Helps me think."

"Okay. What books do you like to read? I like reading books on economics and business."

"I like fiction. Mysteries and thrillers."

"That's interesting. I don't really have time to read for pleasure because I'm swamped with homework and studying. I try to read the newspaper every night."

"What kind of lawyer would you like to be?"

He leans back and seems glad I asked this question. "I'm not sure. I do have an accounting degree, so maybe a tax attorney."

"Oh, cool. We have something in common!"

He stares at me for a second, then laughs, his cheeks growing pink.

I made him laugh. That's good. Things were strained in the beginning, but maybe they'll be better now.

"What are your hobbies?" I ask.

"I like playing sports. Basketball. I try to get together with some of my friends at the gym at least once a week. I love to bake."

I raise my eyebrows. "You love to bake. I love to eat baked

goods. It's perfect."

That makes him laugh again.

"What's your favorite thing to bake?" I ask.

"Cheesecake."

"Mmm. Cheesecake is yum."

"Once someone tastes mine, nothing will ever compare again."

"I can't wait to try it one day," I say.

He smiles a real smile.

I feel so much more comfortable around him now. "I really love programming mobile games. I guess that's my true passion. It's my dream to one day make a living off of it. But I know that's not easy. Maybe with Hashem's help, I will be able to do that one day."

His eyebrows crease. "Games? Like Angry Birds?"

"Yeah. Do you play it?"

He shakes his head. "I never made it past level two. I guess I'm not much of a player."

"That's okay. Not everyone loves games. I mean, I love designing them more than playing them. I don't know if that's weird, though."

His eyebrows crease more. "So...you said you want to

make a living off your games?"

I nod, probably too vehemently. I can't help it. My previous boss told me my whole face gets animated when I talk about programming.

"But what about your family?" he asks.

"What do you mean?"

"Will you always have your nose buried in your games, neglecting your family?"

"What? No way. Family comes first. Always."

That seems to satisfy him, because his face relaxes and he leans back. "Okay."

We both get quiet. My shoes tap on the floor.

"Do you want a drink?" he asks.

"Sure. Thanks."

He gives me a small smile before walking away. My shoes continue to tap on the floor. I have no idea if this is going well or not. I mean, first dates are supposed to be awkward and confusing, not to mention nerve-wracking. But I can't tell if he's having a good time. As for me, I think things are going pretty okay. He seems like a good guy, and I'd like to get to know him better.

When he returns with our drinks, we start talking about

many things, like how we spent the *Sukkos* holiday and where we've traveled to. This might be me being too hopeful, but he doesn't seem weirded out by me. He seems comfortable.

We continue talking about the things going on in our community and our favorite childhood memories. When he glances at his watch, his eyes widen. "Wow, it's past eleven."

My own eyes widen. "Oh, wow. I guess time really *does* fly when you're having fun." Ugh, why did I say that?

He smiles. "It does."

Wait. Does that mean he's having a good time? Does he like me?

"Maybe we should head back," he says.

"Good idea."

We talk more in the car, and before I can blink, he stops in front of my house.

"I had fun," he says as he walks me to the door.

"Me, too."

"Good night, Adina."

"Good night."

He gets into his car and drives away. The door flies open to reveal Mom. "You were out long! Did you have fun?"

"Were you sitting by the window all night?" I ask as I close the door behind me.

"Not all night," she says. "Just the past hour."

I can't help but smile.

"So…?" she asks.

I feel the smile growing wider. "I think it went really well."

Mom's entire face lights up like I told her the greatest news ever. She claps her hands. "That's wonderful. I think I'll have to start going on a diet so I can fit into a gown."

My cheeks burn. "Mom!" I wish she wouldn't get so hopeful. She always does when a date goes well, but I've never made it past a second one. I can't stand disappointing her again.

She leans forward to press a quick kiss on my forehead. "Have faith, Adina."

"I do. I know Hashem will send me my soulmate when the time is right." But all the same, I don't plan on knocking down the armor I've built around myself. Not until I'm one hundred percent sure the right guy has fallen into my path.

"I'll call Mrs. Shain soon and tell her you want to see Yossi again."

"Okay."

I head to my room. Off with the earrings. Off with the necklace. The rings. Off with the contacts and hello to my glasses. I like them—they make me feel sophisticated.

An hour later, Mom enters my room. "Mrs. Shain hasn't heard back from Yossi yet."

A sinking filling enters my stomach.

Mom plays with my hair. "You know that doesn't mean anything. It's late. She'll probably hear from him tomorrow."

"Okay. I'm going to bed."

"Good night, sweetie."

Chapter Five

Today is Friday, the eve of the Sabbath. That means we only work half a day.

I'm sitting at the front desk that has become mine, working on bank statements. Miriam showed me how to use the program yesterday. It's similar to the one I used at my last job. I've officially finished filing, though it's still my job whenever a document needs to be filed.

I glance at Yehoshua's office. I don't know if he's in there because I almost came late today because the bus got stuck behind a truck. Mr. Markus told us to start the project three days ago, and Yehoshua hasn't said anything to me. Maybe that's because he hasn't finished his other work yet. He did say that the due dates are next week, and I guess I hoped he'd finish before then. I'm looking forward to working on that client. I guess I want to prove to both father and son that I'm a good worker and that they can give me more responsibilities. A part of me worries that Yehoshua sees me as an incompetent person because of the grape soda incident.

At 10:00, the front door opens and Yehoshua walks in. I've only worked here a week, and every day he came late. I guess that's one of the perks of being the boss's son. I'm the first person people see when they come in, but Yehoshua doesn't look at me. He just says good morning to everyone before making his way toward his office. I can't help but feel disappointed. I really want to start working on the new client.

My thoughts shift to other things, like Yossi Friedlander. I still haven't heard back from Mrs. Shain. I try to block out the negative thoughts swarming my mind—that he's not interested, or else he would have called the matchmaker. I need to stay hopeful.

Yehoshua walks into the main room. I perk up, waiting for him to ask me to meet him in his office or the conference room. But he just passes by and heads to the copy machine. Once he's finished, he returns to his office without glancing my way. I tell myself to relax. Clearly, he's still not finished with the companies he's working on.

That Special Someone

The rest of the morning goes by at the blink of an eye, and we start packing up. Before I leave, I contemplate going over to Yehoshua and asking him when we're going to work on the new client. I don't want to seem too eager. But then again, maybe he's so busy he forgot? Maybe I can talk to the client and start the work?

I make my way to his office. The door to Mr. Markus's office, which is right next to his, opens and Yehoshua comes out.

"Hey, um—"

"My father's a bit busy now, so maybe it's not the greatest time to talk to him. He threw me out the door. Literally." He grins.

He has a really nice smile. I've noticed it before, but it really is nice.

"Good Shabbos," he says before walking off.

I blink. "Wait!"

It's too late. He's in the bathroom.

I can wait for him to come out, but that would seem weird. Stalkerish. I guess there's always Monday.

***

My sister, Henny, and her family are already at my house

when I get home. They're staying over for Shabbos. Five-year-old Akiva runs to me the second I step through the door. I gather him in my arms and hug him tight. "Look at you! You're so big. Soon I won't be able to hold you anymore."

He giggles.

Someone tugs on my skirt. Four-year-old Tehila. "Hey, sweetie."

"Am I getting big?"

"You're even bigger than Akiva!"

She giggles, too.

Henny walks in, balancing baby Penina on her hip. "Hey."

"Hey." I hug her and tickle Penina.

Since it's almost time for candle lighting, which will start Shabbos, the family is busy with last-minute preparations. I write down the few ideas I thought about for my game on the way home from work, then put away all the things I'm not allowed to touch on Shabbos.

Henny has already given the kids baths, and Mom is in there now. We only have one bathroom. My brother-in-law, Dov, is reading on his iPad.

It's hectic like always, but we all manage to be showered and ready when it's time to light the candles. The mothers of the house are usually the ones who light. Mom and Henny have set theirs up on the table. We watch silently as they wave their hands over the flames and cover their faces, reciting the blessing. I have Tehila in my arms, and she keeps twitching, wanting me to lower her to the floor. But I know she'll run to her mother and I don't want to disturb her. Not to mention I don't want Tehila near the candles.

Once they're finished, Dov leaves to the synagogue and the women gather in the living room. We'll pray in a few minutes, but before then, we spend some time updating each other on what's going on in our lives. Other than my new job, nothing has changed for me.

Henny tells us some funny stories about her kids. I'm not necessarily jealous that she has a family while I'm still single. I do want to be a mom, but I can't even wrap my head around that because there is no guy in the picture. Maybe once I meet the right one, I can start thinking about having kids of my own. But for now, I'm happy to be the fun aunt.

We say the prayers, and once we're done, Henny looks at me. I know that look. She's going to ask me about my dating life. It seems she and I have nothing to talk about these days other than my single status. We used to be really close.

"So how's dating going, Adina?" she asks.

"Fine."

Her eyes move between me and Mom. "Is she seeing anyone seriously?"

Mom shakes her head.

"Has she ever dated anyone seriously before?"

"Why are you asking Mom when I'm sitting right here?"

"I'm sorry. I don't want to say anything hurtful."

"Well, to answer your question: no, I haven't even been on a third date."

"Why?"

I shrug. "Let me know when you have the answer."

She shifts the baby to her other arm. "You know, a friend of mine had a sister who was struggling with dating. She took a class—well, it's not really a class. There's a woman who coaches singles on dating. What the right thing to say is, how to make a good impression. That sort of thing."

I narrow my eyes. "I don't need a dating coach."

"Obviously you do if you can't get a third date."

I fold my arms over my chest and force myself to keep quiet.

"And maybe I can take you shopping to find some decent

clothes."

I stare down at my outfit, which is a white shirt with a black floral design, and a black skirt. "What's wrong with my clothes?"

She doesn't say anything. Then, "They're a little outdated, aren't they?"

"No."

"How old are they? Three years? Five years?"

Well…yeah.

"Don't be stubborn, Adina. That skirt is faded."

I touch it. Maybe it *is* a little faded, but that's only because this skirt is one of my favorites. And I look really pretty in it, if I may say so myself.

"Her clothes are fine," Mom says. "She just needs to figure out how to get guys interested enough to see her again. We still haven't heard back from the Friedlander boy."

I stand up. "I'm going to my room."

"Don't leave, sweetie. We love you and want to help."

"I'm in the middle of a very important chapter in my book," I lie.

They call after me, but I ignore them and shut the door to my room, crawling into bed. I scoot back until I'm leaning against the wall and bring my knees to my chest, wrapping my arms around them. Pressing my cheek into my knees, I try to block out my sister's words. I know she cares about me and wants to see me happily married, but she always upsets me. She married the second person she dated and doesn't understand what it's like to date guy after guy and not meet the right one. She told me countless times that I'm too picky, but how can that be true when ninety percent of the time the guys were the ones who rejected me? She tried to change my look a few times, advising me to straighten my hair and ditch my glasses for contacts. But that hasn't yielded any positive results, either.

Maybe I'm just not meant to have a man in my life. My dad walked out on me fifteen years ago, why should a potential husband be any different?

Before I can stop myself, I spring off my bed and fall down to my knees in front of the bottom drawer of my dresser. Buried beneath the mountain of socks is a sacred picture, one I keep hidden but love dearly. I push aside the piles of socks and my fingers close around the photo. After shutting my eyes for a second and taking a deep breath, I pull it out.

It's a picture of my dad standing next to me in front of an amusement park. I was ten years old. My father surprised me by pulling me out of school so he and I could spend the whole day together. That was the day before he walked out of my life. I haven't heard from him since.

I cried myself to sleep practically every night for a whole year. I blamed myself for him leaving, thinking I did or said something wrong when we hung out. I begged my mom to tell me where he went and when he was coming back. She didn't have any answers. It wasn't until I was thirteen that I realized he would never return. At eighteen, I knew I'd never see him again.

When I was a kid, I thought my dad was the most amazing man in the world. Now, I know he's nothing but a loser.

Tears splat on the photo, mixing in with the ones that have been absorbed into it over the past fifteen years. My siblings have been greatly affected by my dad's walking out, but for some reason, I've been the most affected. Maybe because he and I were the closest in our family. He was a lot like me— quiet, awkward, and we were the only ones in the family who wore glasses. We were almost like best friends.

Programming was the thing that got me through the years. I used to stay in my room all night, learning how to code. That's probably why I suck in the social department.

I push aside some more socks in the drawer and lay the picture inside. Then I cover it with the socks. Mom doesn't know I have the picture. We haven't mentioned my father in over ten years.

Not wanting to think about this any longer, I return to my bed with my book. I'll try to squeeze in some reading before Dov returns from *shul.*

Chapter Six

Mom is still home when I come downstairs on Monday morning. I know something's wrong. She's sitting at the table, her fingers wrapped around a coffee mug.

"Why aren't you at the hospital?" I ask. She works as a nurse.

"I asked my supervisor if I could come in a little later today."

Dread nestles in my stomach. Her eyes look extremely sad. "What happened?" I ask.

She pats the chair next to her. I sit. "Mrs. Shain called last night," she says. "You were busy working on your game, and I didn't want to disturb you."

I stare at the floor. "He said no."

When she doesn't respond, I lift my eyes to hers. They hold

nothing but sadness.

"It's…" I clear my throat. "It's fine." It's not at all, really. I thought the date went pretty well. Yossi seemed to enjoy himself. But I need to be strong, for my mother. "I'll meet the right one at the right time," I continue. "With Hashem's help."

She takes my hands and squeezes them. "With Hashem's help."

"Did Mrs. Shain say why he said no?"

She hesitates.

"I can handle it, Mom. I need all the feedback I can get."

It appears like she doesn't want to tell me, doesn't want to hurt me. But I can learn something important that may make my next date more successful. She must realize that, too, because she says, "He said he had a good time and that you're a great girl. But he doesn't think the two of you would work out."

"Why?"

She sighs. "He said your interests seem to be…different from his. And that he's looking for someone more serious."

"Someone more serious? That's code for he thinks I'm too immature. And he thinks I'm boring."

"Adina—"

I stand. "I need to get to work." I turn to leave, but she doesn't let go of my hand. I look at her. "What?"

"Keep your chin up, okay? I love you."

"I love you, too. And I'm okay."

She kisses the top of my head. "Okay."

When I'm at the door, I stop and turn around. "Maybe I should go shopping with Henny. Maybe...maybe my clothes are too outdated."

"You always dress beautifully, honey."

I adjust the strap of my bag over my shoulder. "I don't know anything anymore." I open the door and walk out.

On the bus ride to work, I play a game to distract myself—not one I designed. I'm not in the mood of playing one of mine. When I reach my stop, I internally groan. I'm not in the mood for work, either. I just want to stay home and be by myself.

As I'm hanging up my jacket, Miriam passes by and smiles. "Hey, good morning. How was Shabbos?"

"Good. Yours?"

"It was really good! I was invited to my in-laws. My mother-in-law is such an amazing cook." She shakes her head. "I won't ever be able to compete with her. But my husband never complains about my cooking." She laughs.

"Sounds great," I mutter.

She keeps her eyes on me for a few seconds. "Is everything okay?"

Sure, everything is awesome. I just got rejected by a guy with whom I had a good date with. He didn't even give me a fair chance. I don't think I'm a boring person. I mean, am I?

"Um, Adina?"

I blink. "Sorry. I'm just tired." Tired of dating.

"The Monday blues," she says as we head to our desks. "Yeah, I feel the same way almost every Monday. But for some reason, I'm in a really good mood this morning."

I force a smile, hoping a fake one will cause me to have a real one. "Maybe it'll rub off on me."

The other girls start arriving, filling the office with chatter. Mr. Markus comes out of his office to wish us a good morning. A few minutes later, the front door opens and Yehoshua rushes in, past my desk and into his office, not saying a word to anyone.

I glance at Miriam, but she doesn't seem shocked. "He's a little weird sometimes," she whispers. "Faigy says he would have been fired on his first day if his dad wasn't the boss, but I don't believe that. Despite his behavior, he's really smart and a hard worker."

"Maybe we shouldn't talk about him," I mumble. Ugh, why do I have this need to defend him? Because he didn't make me feel bad about soiling his shirt? *It doesn't mean anything.*

"Yeah, you're right." Miriam turns back to her desk and starts typing.

Should I go to his office and ask him if I can start working on the new client? I feel like I need to get things moving. I was ready to speak to him on Friday, but I don't feel as confident today. Maybe it's because of Yossi Friedlander.

An hour later, Mr. Markus leaves the office with his son, telling us they'll be back in a few hours. It doesn't take too long for the atmosphere to change. The boss is out—it's time to party.

Miriam rolls over to my desk with a bag of candy, offering me some. "Thanks," I tell her, popping one into my mouth.

"Are you going to the wedding?" she asks.

"What wedding?"

"Mr. Markus's daughter's."

"Oh. He didn't invite me."

"Of course he did. He invited the whole office." She points

to an invitation hanging on the bulletin board.

"Oh."

"It's sort of mandatory," she says, munching on some of the candy.

"Yeah." Shaindy slides onto my desk and takes a few pieces of candy. "He makes it seem like you don't have to go, but he really wants you to. His son got married last year and I didn't go. He called me into his office the next day and asked me why I didn't come. He was like so serious. I thought I was going to get fired."

"You mean, I have to go?"

They nod.

I internally groan. I love weddings just as much as the next person. In theory. It's just that ever since I've been "on the market," I find it a little difficult to enjoy the ceremony. Not only because I'm single, but because of all the women watching me. One thing that's great about our community is how everyone jumps at the opportunity to help one another, especially when it comes to dating. But sometimes, their well-wishes just make things worse.

"When is it?"

"Wednesday night."

That Special Someone

"Great," I mutter.

Miriam laughs.

"I need to think of an outfit and do my hair." I groan.

Miriam laughs again. "You make it seem like you don't go to many weddings."

My cheeks heat up and I avert my gaze to the bank statements on my desk. "Well, I don't go to many. Basically all my friends are married."

"That's so nice," Miriam says. "I know many people our age that are still single—practically half my graduating class."

"I've been out of high school for two years," Shaindy says, "and only fifteen girls from my grade are either engaged or married. *Fifteen* out of *one hundred*."

I wish we wouldn't talk about this.

"Really sad," Miriam says. "I hope they all find their intended soon. You too, Adina and Shaindy."

Shaindy blushes and says a quiet thank you. I mumble one, too. It's not that I'm trying to be rude, it's just that the phrase "I hope you find your intended soon" is what all the married people say to the single ones. Yes, it's a blessing, but it doesn't make the single person feel good.

"There's more to life than marriage, you know." The words

fly out of my mouth before I can stop them.

Both Miriam and Shaindy gape at me like I told them I'm really a guy dressed up as a girl.

"What?" Shaindy asks.

"I mean, of course marriage is important," I start babbling. "One of the most important parts of life. But there's nothing wrong with being single."

Naomi, Michal, and Faigy have gathered around my desk.

"So you don't want to get married?" Naomi asks, her nostrils flared.

"Of course I do! But I don't want to feel like I'm a second-class citizen because I'm not wearing a *sheitel*, you know."

"If you have that attitude, you'll never get married," Naomi says.

All the girls stare at her. Then Miriam lightly slaps her arm. "That wasn't very nice."

She folds her arms. "I just mean that it's hard. Everyone needs to put all their effort into finding the right person. If you're lazy about it, you'll never get married."

"She does have a point," Faigy says. "My cousin is in his late forties. He kept pushing dating off, saying he had time. Now it's too late."

That Special Someone

"It's never too late," I say. "I'm sure he'll meet someone."

"Maybe," Naomi says, her nostrils flared again. "But it wouldn't be easy."

I really don't want to talk about this. I don't even know why I brought this up. Did I *have* to open my big mouth? I guess I'm just sick and tired of always being looked at a little differently because I'm not married.

I take out my phone and start playing the level of my game. Thankfully, the girls start talking about something else.

Chapter Seven

Avigayil calls me when I'm on my way home from work and asks if I can help her with an arts and crafts project she's creating for her preschool students. Instead of going off at my usual stop, I stay on the bus until I'm in her area and walk the few blocks to her house. As soon as she opens the door, she flings her arms around me like I'm her life savior.

"I'm in way over my head," she says as she drags me up to her room, not even giving me a chance to say hello to her parents. I feel my jaw practically drop to the floor when I see the mess. Construction paper, paint, markers, glitter, scissors, and many other items are scattered around.

"Wow," I say.

"I know, right? Here I was, thinking I can be so creative and artistic. And all I've done is destroy my room."

That Special Someone

"Well, why did you call me over? I'm the most uncreative person in the world."

She folds her arms over her chest. "Am I not standing before a girl who spends all her free time *designing* games?"

I feel my cheeks flush. "You know all the art I know is self-taught. I'm not even good."

She clicks her tongue. "Again with the pessimism. Just get on the floor and help me come up with some project, or else I may not live to be at my own wedding."

I laugh as I settle down on the floor. She and I start to brainstorm different ideas. Since the kids are in the middle of learning about animals at the zoo, we'll draw different animals on paper that we'll give out to the girls. They will paste the papers over construction paper and cut out the animals in whatever color they choose.

As I'm drawing an elephant, I say, "Yossi Friedlander said no."

Avigayil stops cutting out a lion, her face full of sympathy. "I'm sorry. He doesn't deserve you if he doesn't see what a wonderful person you are."

"Thanks. I needed to hear that."

"Are there any other boys brewing?"

I shake my head. Then Yehoshua Markus's face pops into my mind. I quickly shake my head again, trying to toss him away. He hardly looks my way at work. I bet the only thing he thinks about when he thinks about me—if he even does—is that I'm the girl who ruined his expensive shirt.

"What?" Avigayil asks, her eyes suspicious.

"What?"

"You're blushing and muttering to yourself. There *is* a guy brewing, isn't there?"

I hold out my palms. "No, there isn't. But…"

"But what?" She's practically bouncing, her eyes bright with intrigue.

"You know the guy who works with me? My boss's son?"

She nods.

"Well, um…"

Her eyes turn even brighter. "Oh my gosh! Do you like him?"

"No," I quickly say. "I don't. I mean…" I release some air. "Don't laugh at me, okay?"

"Why would I laugh at you?"

"Because I'm about to tell you a Classic Adina story."

She rests her elbow on her knee and balances her chin on

her hand. "I'll try my hardest."

Not meeting her gaze, I tell her about the grape soda incident. Then I hesitantly raise my eyes to her. I know she's trying really hard not to laugh because her cheeks are red and puffed up. I wave my hand. "Let it out. I know you need to get it out of your system."

She bursts into giggles.

"I know," I mutter. "I went from having a pretty awful first day to having a disastrous second one."

She shakes her head as she fights off the giggles. "I'm telling you, Adina. There are many guys out there who find clumsy girls endearing and attractive. You just have to meet one."

I don't say anything.

She wipes her eyes. "So how did Yehoshua Markus react?"

"Well…" I scratch the side of my neck as I get all twitchy. "He seemed…okay with it. I thought he would have gotten upset or maybe send me the cleaning bill. But he was so cool about it." I shake my head. "I don't know."

"So you like him because he didn't make you feel bad."

"Yeah, I guess."

Her eyes are still bright. "Do you think he likes you back?"

"No. He hardly looks at me. And we're supposed to do a project together and he hasn't said a single word to me about it. I think he's avoiding me." I grab another piece of paper and start drawing a tiger. "It doesn't matter. I can never be with a guy like him, anyway."

"What do you mean?"

"I'm awkward. Quiet. I like to sit in the corner and observe. He seems like the kind of guy who would want a girl who is the life of the party. Someone outgoing. And he's so put together and charismatic." I hold out my hands. "Just look at me. I look like I got dressed in the dark."

She snorts. "Please."

"Do you think I should buy better clothes?"

Her forehead wrinkles as she scans me from top to bottom. "What's wrong with your clothes?"

"Henny said they're outdated. She thinks they have something to do with the fact that I can never get past a second date."

"You always look great, Adina. Modest but attractive. Don't worry about it."

My tiger looks like a cat. I crumple the paper into a ball and toss it somewhere.

That Special Someone

"Thanks for helping me, by the way," she says. "You're such a good friend."

I smile. "Thanks."

We work in silence, until Mrs. Miller enters with refreshments.

"It's okay, Mom." Avigayil takes the tray from her and lays it on the floor. "I was planning on getting something later."

"It's my pleasure to serve you girls," she says, sitting down on Avigayil's bed. "Once the two of you are married, I'll miss it."

"Thanks, Mrs. Miller," I say.

"No problem. How is your mother doing?"

"*Baruch Hashem*, well."

"I'm glad to hear that. And how are you? Avigayil tells me you started a new job."

"Yeah, I really like it."

"I'm glad to hear that, too."

We talk for a few minutes before Mrs. Miller leaves. Avigayil and I continue working in silence until I say, "It seems that the only thing girls our age talk about is dating and marriage."

Her eyebrows are scrunched in concentration as she draws

a giraffe. When she messes it up, she groans, crumples up the paper, and tosses it into the pile of discarded drawings. "Well, that's the most important thing in our lives right now. It's constantly on our minds."

"I wish it didn't have to be like that, though. I wish we didn't have to be looked at differently because we're still single."

Avigayil shrugs. "It's just the way it is. Marriage is the upmost important thing to a *frum* Jew. We just have to endure it until we get married."

"Speaking of which," I say. "How's it going with Shmuli Lerer? Did you guys go out again?"

"Excuse me, we haven't finished discussing Yehoshua Markus."

I sigh. "There's nothing to discuss. I'm just a desk to him. No, worse than a desk. I'm a small paperclip."

She laughs. "Maybe that's for the best. The last thing you need is to get involved with someone at work. Things might be a bit awkward, especially if it doesn't work out."

She's right. After all, the girl who worked there before me had to quit because she dated him and it didn't go well. I'm very thankful for my job and don't want to leave.

That Special Someone

"Okay, so let's talk about Shmuli," I say.

Her cheeks turn dark red. "We haven't had the chance to go out again because he's swamped with school, but we've spoken on the phone a few times. We were up until midnight last night."

"That's great. It's good that you have things to talk about."

"I was thinking the same thing! We could have spoken for hours, but he was the mature one and suggested we say goodnight. If I marry him, at least I know he'll be responsible."

He really does sound like a good guy. I'm not jealous of Avigayil—I mean, of course I am a little jealous, but my happiness for her triumphs over that. It would be awesome to see her settle down with a good guy. It would be awesome if *I* can settle down with a good guy, too. Hopefully sooner rather than later.

Avigayil lays the animals on the floor. "Hey, these look amazing."

I scoot closer to get a better look. "So cute!"

"I'll paste two or three on a page and make copies at school. The kids will love pasting them on the construction paper and cutting them out. And we can use googly eyes!" She puts her arms around me. "Thanks so much. I would be lost without you."

"I think I just got an idea for my game," I say, my wheels starting to spin.

"Really? That's great! Now we both gained something."

I grab my bag and rummage inside for my special notebook and a pen. I start scribbling things down.

"When are you going to finish the game?" Avigayil asks. "I can't wait to play it."

"I can't wait to finish it." I close my notebook and drop it back in my bag. "Yossi Friedlander claimed making mobile games are a waste of time. Do you think all guys would feel the same?"

"I don't think so. I think it's really cool."

"My coworkers think I'm crazy for loving it so much. Sometimes I wonder if I'm the strange one, or if they are."

She chuckles. "Them, definitely."

I join in the laughter.

"Okay," she says. "Let's clean this place up."

Chapter Eight

Neither Mr. Markus nor Mr. Markus Junior has arrived yet, which is the reason my coworkers are chatting and not working. It's also the reason why I'm working on the character design for my game.

Naomi claims they both won't come in today because Mr. Markus's daughter's wedding is tomorrow night. When I have a need to design or program, I just *have* to get it out of my system. And anyway, I'll soon be done with the bank statements and I'll have nothing to do. Miriam told me that Mr. Markus gets upset when he sees his employees not working, and the last thing I want is my boss being upset with me after only a week at this job.

"That's so cute!"

I look up and realize Miriam rolled over to me, her gaze on

the fish I'm drawing. "Cute?" I ask, feeling a frown on my face. "It's not supposed to be cute." I fold the paper and put it in my bag. I never throw out any of my drawings because I never know when I might need them for another game.

"Really?" she asks. "I thought that game is for kids."

"Well, I'd like it to be for all ages. But I suck at drawing."

"It looked really good, though. Maybe you can use it if you ever design a kids' game."

I give her a sincere smile. Unlike most of my other coworkers, Miriam seems to be interested in my game design.

She rolls closer to me. "Hey, you're hearing suggestions, right?"

I glance at the others. They're deep in a discussion. I nod to Miriam.

"Okay. My husband has a friend who is a really good guy. He's going for his PhD in psychology and he likes playing sports and he loves kids. He's really great!"

At the prospect of a new guy, a new potential husband, a part of me gets excited. Imagine finally meeting the one! But then the other part of my feels dejected. Another potential rejection.

"Can you email me his profile?" I ask.

"Yes, definitely!"

"Thanks."

She rubs my arm. "Hey, cheer up. You'll meet the right guy soon."

"Was I scowling?"

"Yeah."

"Oh. I didn't mean to."

"It's okay. I met my husband two years ago, but it was very tough for me, too. Believe me, it'll all be worth it."

"That's what they say."

"It's true," she assures me. "And do you want to know what I once heard by a speech? The speaker said that the longer it takes for you to find your soulmate, the more you'll appreciate him because you had to work harder for him. It's sort of like your game programming. The harder you work on it, the more you appreciate it. Right?"

I think about her words for a few seconds. I've been working on my game for years. When I finish it—if I ever do— it'll feel like such a big accomplishment.

"That's actually really nice," I tell her. "Thanks for telling me."

"I want to help as much as I can," she says. "Most married

people forget what it was like when they were single. They always promise themselves when they're still single that when they finally get married, they'll do whatever they can to help their unmarried friends. But that doesn't really happen. They forget what it's like."

"Yeah." My leg twitches. "Don't you think girls our age have other things to talk about besides dating and marriage?"

She laughs. "What do you want to talk about?"

I shrug. "I don't know. But I'm getting sick of talking about dating."

She nods. "Okay. I'm sorry."

"No," I quickly say. "I don't mean to offend you or anything. I'm just getting tired of talking about the same thing over and over again. I talk about it with my mom, my unmarried friend. With my sister. And at work."

She nods again. "Yeah, I guess it does get tiresome. And nothing's wrong with being single." She winks.

I laugh.

The door springs open and Yehoshua Markus strides in. The girls rush to their desks and start working. He's not the boss, but I expect he'd tell his dad if he found us not working.

Yehoshua passes by, but then he stops and walks back. He

puts his palms on my desk and leans forward. "My dad didn't come in, right?"

He's talking to me? He's hardly said more than a few words to me since I started working here. And his eyes...they're such a deep brown color. Like dark chocolate.

He raises his eyebrow.

"W-what?" I stammer.

"Did my dad come in?" he asks, his voice patient. "I see his office is locked."

"No," I say. "He didn't come in. It's his daughter's wedding tomorrow night, so it's possible he won't be in today or tomorrow."

Yehoshua's eyes crinkle like he's trying to hold in a laugh. I feel my cheeks burn. Oh my gosh. Of course he knows his sister is getting married tomorrow night! I spoke to Yehoshua as if he was one of our clients.

"Okay," he says. "If he calls, can you transfer him to me? I can't seem to get hold of him and I need to speak to him."

"Sure," I say, my cheeks still warm.

Once Yehoshua disappears into his office, I look at Miriam and see her also holding back a laugh. "I don't know why he makes me so nervous," I say.

She has a knowing smile on her face. "He seems to have that effect on many of the girls here."

I narrow my eyes. "Are you insinuating something?"

"He's difficult, Adina. Just be careful, okay?"

"I don't know what you're getting at," I say, my voice the serious it's ever been. "But it's not what you think."

"I hope so." She turns back to her desk.

I tap my pen on my desk a few times before I roll over to her. "What exactly do you mean he's difficult?"

Miriam sighs and logs out of the tax software. "Suri's not the only one who's had her heart broken by Yehoshua. A close friend of mine went out with him last year. She was so sure he was going to propose to her, but he called things off instead. He led her on for weeks and just dumped her."

"I'm sure there's more to it than that."

"He's a good person. A great coworker. Crazy smart. But he's just not very sensitive to other people's feelings. I hope he learns to be more sympathetic, or else I don't know if he'll ever get married."

Not that I was even contemplating dating him or anything, but it would be best to not get involved with him. Not that he would ever dream of getting involved with me, anyway.

That Special Someone

During lunch, I take out my phone and play the level I designed. I must have played it a million times, but I always seem to find something wrong or a way to improve it. It's the little details that matter. The expression on the character's face, the scenery. I don't realize someone standing in front of my desk until he clears his throat.

I raise my eyes and find Yehoshua standing there. "Do you want to start on Mr. Greene?"

"Huh?"

"Didn't my father tell you we'd work on a new client together?"

"Yeah! Of course. I've been waiting all this time."

His eyebrows furrow. "You have? Oh, I'm sorry. I'm having some problems with Yitzy's Plumbing, which is why I need to speak to my dad urgently. But apparently, he's off the grid and I have no way of getting hold of him."

"Did you try his cell?"

He runs his hand through his dark brown hair. "Done that and left him a gazillion voicemails. Do you want to start working on Mr. Greene? I'll file an extension for Yitzy's Plumbing. Maybe my father will be more present once the wedding's over. It's been stressing him out."

"Weddings tend to do that," Miriam says with a grin.

"Yeah, they do," I say. "Not that I have experience or anything…unless you count my siblings' weddings, but…never mind." I need to stop babbling. "Um. Should I come to your office?"

"Yeah. But can we meet in half an hour? I'm taking my lunch now."

"Yeah. Sure."

Finally! I'm ready to start some real work. But the prospect of working alone with Yehoshua Markus makes me so nervous. I don't know why. It's not because he was nice when I spilled the grape soda on him, right? I've already established that he was just being nice. It's not because of his pretty eyes, either, or the way he laughed when I made a complete fool of myself this morning. He didn't seem put off by me, just amused. In a good way.

Nah, I must have just imagined it. He probably thinks I'm strange.

"You're muttering to yourself," Miriam says, laughter in her voice.

"That tends to happen when I have too many thoughts in my head," I say. "Have you ever worked on a project with

That Special Someone

Yehoshua?"

She shakes her head. "I don't think any of us have."

"Why am I, then?"

She shrugs. "Yehoshua mostly keeps to himself. Maybe Mr. Markus wants him to get more involved with the others."

But why do I have to be the guinea pig? Ah, who am I kidding? I want to be the guinea pig. I shake my head. No, that's not true. Yehoshua Markus is difficult. D-I-F-F-I-C-U-L-T.

I don't really do anything for the next half hour, just sit at my desk and eat my lunch. I'm too nervous to work on my game. When Yehoshua returns, I sit straight. Our eyes meet, and he nods to me before tilting his head toward his office. I return the nod.

After gathering some paper and a pen, I stand up.

"Good luck," Miriam wishes.

"Thanks."

As I walk around my desk, I catch sight of Naomi watching me, daggers in her eyes. I ignore her and head toward Yehoshua's office. The door is closed. After telling myself to relax and taking a deep breath, I close my fingers over the knob and pull the door open. He's sitting at his desk, typing on his computer. I keep the door slightly ajar before taking a few hesitant steps in.

He doesn't look at me but keeps his eyes pasted on the screen. I guess he's too engrossed in whatever he's doing. I stand there awkwardly, debating if I should sit down. He hasn't told me to, but this *is* a meeting, isn't it?

When he's finally finished writing what looks like an email, he turns to me. "Oh. Please sit."

I do.

He opens a folder and pulls out papers. "This is all the info Mr. Greene gave us on his companies. He has five. My dad wasn't kidding when he said they're a mess."

"Okay."

"So you can start off by putting his companies' info into the program. Did anyone show you how to use it?"

I nod.

"Once you put them in and print out the statements, maybe we'll be able to make sense of what's going on. If you have any questions, you can call or email him. Or you can ask me."

"Okay."

"Look them over and see if you have any questions."

I take the papers from him and leaf through them. He's

right—they *are* a mess. It'll take forever to sort through everything.

"So...how do you like working here so far?" he asks.

"It's great! Your dad is really nice and the girls are great, too."

He nods. "So I've been told."

I drop my eyes to the papers and quickly flip through them, keeping myself busy.

"Accounting isn't your true passion, is it?"

I glance up. "What?"

He leans back in his chair. "Accounting." He yawns. "I know that's not what you really love. I mean, who does?"

"It's not that bad. It's very challenging at times."

He leans forward and looks into my face. "Does your true passion have anything to do with what you do at your desk during your break? You're always bent over your phone and jotting things down in your little notebook."

He noticed that? I thought he never paid attention to me.

"Maybe my true passion is accounting," I say. "How do you know it's not? Not everyone finds it boring."

His eyes circle over face. "Trust me, I know it's not. C'mon. What's your secret?" His eyes are filled with curiosity and intrigue. I'm not sure if he's trying to tease me.

"I program mobile games," I say.

He just stares at me. "You what?"

"Games for the phone."

"You're saying you actually create them?"

I nod. "The design and the programming."

He continues to stare at me. "Wow. I wasn't expecting that at all."

I swallow. "What were you expecting?"

"I don't know. The things girls are usually into it. But making games? That's the coolest thing I've ever heard."

My heart starts to race. "Really?" No guy has ever said that to me before.

"Yeah. What are you working on now?"

"Oh. Um, it's silly."

"Try me."

I look at him for a bit, debating if he's seriously interested or just messing with me. He seems sincere. "It's about a girl who enters a magical world. She meets many different kinds of people and creatures there and she needs to help them. And the main quest is that she needs to find her way home. It's silly, right?"

That Special Someone

"Not at all. It sounds fascinating. You sound fascinating."

Did he...? I feel my entire face heat up. "Y-you don't think it's a waste of time?"

"What? Making games? I see the fire you have in your eyes when you talk about it. I can tell it's something you really love. Why would it be a waste of time if it makes you happy?"

My thoughts exactly. I just blink at him, not believing what's going on right now.

"Can I see it?" he asks.

"No, no. Not until I'm done."

He frowns. "Okay. But as soon as you're done, I want to be the first person to play it."

"I don't think that'll happen any time soon."

"Why? Are people telling you not to do it because it's a waste of time?"

"Wouldn't your parents tell you that?"

He thinks for a second. "Hmm. Yeah. I wouldn't listen to them, though. If it's something I love, I'd do it no matter what. You're kind of my inspiration."

"W...what?"

He shakes his head. "Sorry." He picks up his pen and doesn't look at me. Then, "So you'll look over Greene's papers?"

Right. Work. I nod.

"Okay. Let me know if you have any questions."

I walk out of his office in a complete daze and sit at my desk, staring at the computer screen. What happened in Yehoshua's office? He's the first person I've met who thinks my programming is actually cool. And he noticed me sitting at my desk when I thought he didn't think twice about me. What does all of this mean?

It's not until I'm on the bus ride home that I realize I hadn't asked him what his true passion is.

Chapter Nine

"Mom, what's wrong with what I'm wearing?" I ask as she sticks herself in my closet and pushes aside shirt after shirt, skirt after skirt.

"It's a *wedding*, Adina. You know you're getting invited to less and less weddings since almost all of your friends are married. You need to look your best. You never know who will be there."

I refrain from rolling my eyes. She's referring to matchmakers or mothers of potential boys. Since women tend to dress their finest at weddings, it's the perfect opportunity to catch someone's attention. I don't really like this because I don't think a wedding is the right place to get a date—I mean, I'm attending the wedding to celebrate the union between two people. But you never know where your husband might come from. One should always keep one's options open.

Yehoshua Markus's face flashes before my eyes. He's going to be at the wedding. Will he…notice me?

I shake my head. What does it matter?

He seemed really interested in my programming. Does that mean he's interested in me? Does that mean I need to dress up to impress him?

"How about this?" Mom holds out a pink, ruffled shirt and a black skirt.

"I've worn that to like every wedding."

"It's fine. The people at this wedding weren't at the other ones."

I wonder if Yehoshua would find me pretty in that outfit. I shake my head again. It doesn't matter.

"I'll leave you to get ready," Mom says, her eyes bright.

I want to tell her not to get her hopes up. It's her wish that someone at the wedding will take one look at me and think I'd be perfect for her son. I know she means well, but I'm really getting tired of all of this. I just want to enjoy the wedding without having to worry whether I'm making a good impression.

I get dressed, then put on my contacts. I straightened my

hair earlier, when I got home from work. Once my makeup is applied, I stand before the mirror and study myself. Well, this is as good as it's going to get.

As soon as I go downstairs and step into the kitchen, Mom walks over to examine me. A smile filled with love and pride overtakes her face. Then she frowns. "You forgot your jewelry again?"

I touch my ears and find them bare. "Oh."

She sighs.

"I know. I'm the only girl in the whole world who has a box full of jewelry and never puts any on." I turn around and head upstairs.

After I'm covered in gold, I study myself in the mirror again. The jewelry does make me look prettier.

"Much better," Mom says when I return downstairs. She kisses the top of my head. "You look beautiful. How are you getting to the wedding hall?"

"I can walk. It's not far."

"Okay, but call me when you're ready to come home and I'll pick you up. I don't want you walking out alone so late at night."

I nod. "Thanks."

Chaya T. Hirsch

I don my jacket, wish my mother goodbye, and step into the October cool air. The reception is called for 6:30, and it's nearly 7:00. Weddings never start on time.

The walk only takes twenty minutes. Every time I edge closer to a wedding hall, a nervous-excited jolt travels down my spine. What would it be like when I'm at my own wedding? Will I ever experience it? I'd like to think I'll meet the right guy soon. I need to hope.

I enter the reception area, which is mostly empty. I scan around for a familiar face and find Miriam at the smorgasbord table with a full plate. I walk over and tap her shoulder.

"Adina, hi! You look stunning." She hugs me with one arm since the other one is holding her plate. "I love your straight hair."

"Thanks. You look amazing." I scan around. "Are the other girls here yet?"

"I don't think they're coming for the *chuppah*. They might just come for the dancing."

I take a plate and start piling food on it. One thing I love about weddings is that they're an excuse to stuff your face with delicious food. There are so many choices here—hot dishes, salads, baked goods. Miriam and I sit at one of the tables and eat and talk. When I see Mr. Markus walk into the reception area, I get up to wish him a *mazel tov*.

"*Mazel tov, mazel tov*," he says, his eyes the brightest I've ever seen.

Yehoshua strides in and marches over to his father. "Dad, Mom needs you upstairs." His eyes move to me, and he does a double take. My cheeks warm up. He looks really good, really dashing in a black suit and light blue tie. His hair is nicely combed and his yarmulke sits neatly on his head. I'm about to wish him a *mazel tov*, but he turns around and walks outside, where he rushes up the stairs. The bride is getting ready up there. In a few minutes, she'll join the guests down here.

I'm not too ashamed to get another plate and taste some more food. After a few minutes, the bride comes downstairs and sits in the exquisite chair set aside for her. She looks gorgeous and her gown is dazzling.

"I can't help but think of my wedding whenever I'm at other weddings," Miriam says, munching on sesame chicken.

"What was it like?"

I always seem to ask married people how they felt at their weddings. It's something I'm so curious about.

"Gosh, I was a mess," she says. "The makeup woman was

held up in traffic, in *New Jersey*. I was freaking out because there was no way she would have made it. Thank God my cousin knew someone who was able to rush over in time. And then I couldn't find my bouquet! We looked all over the hall. It turned out my niece took it and pretended to be the bride." She laughs, her eyes far away like she's buried deep in her memories. "I was so *nervous* to actually get married. You have no idea."

"But you were excited, too, right?" I say.

"I think I was too nervous to be excited. But when my husband walked in to pull the veil over my face, I relaxed. I know that's weird—I should have gotten *more* nervous. But looking into his face made me realize how much I loved him and how much I was looking forward to building a life with him and starting a family."

I play with a cherry tomato in my plate. "It sounds wonderful."

"It is," she says in a dreamy voice. "We got the wedding video a few months later. My husband and I would watch it over and over again for weeks." She laughs like she's embarrassed. "I know, we were total nerds."

"No, I think it's sweet. And romantic."

That Special Someone

She reaches out to rub my arm. "You'll experience it, too. God willing."

"Thanks."

I catch Yehoshua coming down the stairs with a woman behind him. She's short and is wearing an exquisite gray gown, and her dark *sheitel* is styled beautifully. I'm guessing she's his mother. They seem to be arguing in hushed whispers. Yehoshua runs his hand through his hair and turns slightly around, then twists back around and throws his hands up. His mother shakes her head and says something. Yehoshua storms to the men's side of the reception area.

"This sesame chicken is delicious, isn't it? I'm getting some more." Miriam dashes to the table.

I continue playing with my cherry tomato, the image of Yehoshua Markus arguing with his mom burning in my skull.

Miriam returns with a plate filled with the sesame chicken and salad. "I have no idea why I'm so hungry. I hope I'm not preg—" She cuts herself off as her eyes widen.

"Wouldn't all the food make you nauseous if you were?" I ask, then immediately regret it. This isn't any of my business.

Miriam blushes, then leans forward. "Honestly? I have no idea. It's been two years already…My mother-in-law is putting this crazy pressure on me."

"I'm sorry."

"Thanks. It's just hard."

"I can imagine. It's like when you're single, everyone puts all this pressure on you to get married. Then if you're married for over a year and don't have a baby yet, they start asking questions, like, 'Nu, when are you going to have a baby already?' I wish people would just mind their own business."

"My husband is their only child," Miriam tells me. "My mother-in-law always looks at my stomach when we visit them."

"Try not to let her bother you. You'll have a baby at the right time, God-willing."

"Thanks." She takes a mouthful of salad. "You know, you're very easy to talk to."

"Thank you."

The music blares. Miriam's head snaps up. "He's coming!" She scrambles to her feet to join the many other women gathering around the bride.

This is the part of the wedding where the groom comes to pull the veil over his bride. It's a tradition we've been doing ever since Lavan tricked our patriarch Yaakov and gave him

That Special Someone

Leah as a wife instead of Rochel. It's a way to ensure that the man is marrying the right woman. I always find this part one of the most romantic things about a wedding. Since it's tradition for the bride and groom to not see each other for a week before the wedding—so they could be overly excited to see each other on their wedding night—this is the first time they will come face to face. Totally romantic.

I don't bother to stand with the others to watch, though. I never get a good view. The only times I was able to see was at my siblings' weddings.

I manage to get a glimpse of the groom. He's pretty good-looking.

Miriam meets me back at the table, and together we head to the *chuppah* ceremony. When I was a kid, this part of the wedding always seemed to drag, since it's basically blessings. But as an adult, it feels like it goes by quite fast. Miriam and I choose seats toward the back.

By some weddings, family members march, while at others only the bride and groom do. At this one, it seems like the family members are marching. My body straightens when Yehoshua walks down the aisle with a teenage girl. I guess she must be his sister. He wears a pleasant expression on his face, and I feel my heart race a little. Then there are two flower girls who are just so adorable, and then the bride marches down the aisle.

The ceremony ends with the groom stomping on a glass cup. Everyone yells, "*Mazel tov!*" and the music blares again. The bride and groom walk up the aisle, their hands clasped together. Another romantic part of the wedding—the bride and groom holding hands for the first time.

When I glance at Miriam, I see she has tears in her eyes. She laughs, embarrassed. "Sorry. I always get emotional during *chuppahs*."

"Did you cry at yours?" I ask.

"Yeah! Everyone kept asking me if I was okay."

The bride and groom will now head to the Yichud Room, where they will be alone together for the first time. The guests will be served their first course. Since Miriam and I were only invited for the *chuppah* and dancing, we sit on the couch in the lobby. We'll join the others once the dancing begins.

We chat for a few minutes before Yehoshua and another man walk into the lobby and sit on the couch across us. I don't know why my face heats up. I guess because I feel a little awkward being in such close proximity to him. I know I was even closer to him yesterday when we worked on the project, but I'm dressed well now. A part of me wonders if he'll look at me, while the other part hopes he doesn't because it'll make me feel so embarrassed.

Miriam doesn't seem to notice me fidgeting. "I wonder when the other girls are coming." She scans her cell phone. "Faigy texted me half an hour ago and told me she'll be here shortly."

The guy Yehoshua is conversing with is speaking very loudly, about a sports team who apparently are not doing well this season. Miriam frowns because she can hardly hear herself talk. I peek at Yehoshua and see his eyes subtly flit to me. I quickly look away. He does, too. My heart starts to pound.

I hope my makeup looks okay. I'm about to get up and go to the bathroom to make sure I look good, but I force myself to remain planted on the couch. It doesn't matter how I look. Nope. Yehoshua is not interested in me. Nope.

"I'm not keeping tabs on them like you are," Yehoshua says to his friend. "I think you need to get a life."

His friend playfully punches his shoulder. "I do have a life, thank you. I think you're the one who needs to get a life."

"I do have a life, thank you," Yehoshua says. His friend

makes a move to wrestle him on the couch, but he pulls back and they both chuckle.

"Guys," I mutter.

"What?" Miriam asks.

"Oh, sorry. I was just talking to myself. About..." I nod my head in their direction. "They're acting like such guys," I whisper. "All that sports talk."

Miriam raises an eyebrow. "And you would know that because you're such an expert on guys?"

I laugh lightly. "Yeah, I dated every single guy on the planet," I say sarcastically. "I know them inside and out."

She laughs.

When I glance at Yehoshua, I find his eyes on me. This time, he doesn't look away. Did he overhear what I just said?

I don't pull my eyes away, either. It's like they're frozen.

He's forced to break his gaze when his friend claps him on the shoulder. "Come, Josh. Let's eat."

Josh. That's so not him. Actually, the more I think about it, the more I realize it suits him perfectly.

The door to the hall opens and Naomi rushes in. Miriam stands and they hug each other. Then they drop down on the couch. "You look so good!" Naomi tells Miriam.

That Special Someone

"You, too!"

All of the sudden, I feel invisible. "Hey, Naomi," I say.

She glances at me. "Hi." Then she returns her attention to Miriam and starts talking about how it took her forever to get her hair done right. I lean back on the couch and stare at my shoes.

That's when I notice Yehoshua is still sitting on the couch across from us. His friend left to the men's section of the main hall. Yehoshua quickly looks away when our eyes meet and stands, walking into the men's section.

"Wow, he looks so good," Naomi says, staring after him.

Back off, my mind yells.

I tell it to hush up.

"Did you see the way he was looking at me?" Naomi says. "He was looking at me, right?"

Miriam looks uncomfortable, shifting in her seat. "Didn't the matchmaker tell you he's not interested?"

She waves her hand. "He told her he thought I was too young. Five years isn't *that* much of a difference, especially when I'm mature. I think he might change his mind."

Miriam doesn't say anything.

"You think I'm being ridiculous," Naomi mutters, the hurt

obvious in her tone. She lowers her gaze to her purse that's sitting on her lap.

Miriam rubs her back. "No. Just…maybe you shouldn't be so hung up on him. You need to move on and meet a good guy. Someone who will treat you well and respect you."

"Yehoshua would," she whispers.

"Why do you like him so much?" I blurt before I can stop myself.

Naomi stares at me like she just notices I'm sitting here and am a real person and not part of the couch. She narrows her eyes. "That's none of your business."

"I know," I say. "But I've been at this dating thing long enough. Maybe I can help you." I bite my lip. I feel like I just threw some meat at a lion.

Her eyes are still narrowed, but then they soften. She's about to say something, then seems to change her mind. She puts her attention back on Miriam. "I just wish I could go out with him," she says. "Just once."

It doesn't seem like Miriam knows what to say. Luckily, she doesn't have to because Faigy and Shaindy arrive. Miriam waves them over. "Hey! I think the dancing will start soon. You both look amazing!"

That Special Someone

They sit down and the four of them start talking. They don't pay attention to me. I guess I don't blame them—I'm still the new girl, and they are a tight group. I get up and go to the bathroom to check how I look. There is no more lipstick on my lips and some of my light blue eyeshadow has smeared off. I'm not one to carry makeup in my bag, since I hardly wear makeup. But I still look okay. Not that it matters. I haven't seen any women scouting me. I'm happy about that because I don't feel as pressured.

When I exit the bathroom, I realize the band is playing the usual dancing music. My coworkers are nowhere to be found. They must have gone into the hall to join in the dancing. I walk in.

Dancing is always fun. Mr. Markus's daughter looks really happy. When this wave is over, the guests, and bride and groom, sit down to eat the next course. The five of us return to the hall. Once again, the girls talk and I'm pushed to the side.

Maybe I should go home. This feels like ninth grade, before I made friends. When I tried so hard to fit in and was just ignored. Maybe I'll never fit in with these girls. Maybe it was a mistake to leave my last job.

"Oh my gosh!" Shaindy sits forward. "Who's singing? He

sounds amazing!"

The four of them dash into the women's section. Unable to hold back my curiosity, I follow them and crowd around the opening of the *mechitza*, partition, to look into the men's section. I stumble back. Yehoshua Markus is holding the mic.

His face is soft and his eyes are slightly closed as he sings. He has so much emotion on his face. Something warm enters my insides. Not only does he have the most amazing voice I've ever heard, but he's putting so much feeling into it. I stand there frozen as he continues to sing. When it's over, I blink and look at the other women gathered around. They look transfixed, too.

The night continues with more eating and more dancing. Michal joins us a little while later. When I feel like I've danced my feet off, I tell the girls I'm heading home. They wish me a good night.

I call my mom to pick me up and wait outside the hall. It's a bit chilly, but not too bad. I fold my arms over my chest and bounce on my heels. Weddings are always a ton of fun, but I feel a little sad when they're over. Depressed. I guess that's normal.

Many of the guests are starting to leave. I check my watch.

That Special Someone

It's past 10 PM. I don't expect Mom to get here that fast.

The door to the hall opens and Yehoshua comes out, followed by a boy who looks about nine years old. They are both laughing. The boy stretches his arm toward Yehoshua, leaping up as he tries to hit the back of his head. But Yehoshua is too tall.

"Grow another few inches," he says, twisting around and ruffling the boy's hair. "I bet you'll grow a foot taller than me."

"Uncle Joshie," the boy says, his voice teasing. He jumps up and tries to hit the back of Yehoshua's head again, but it's futile. Yehoshua is just too tall.

"Don't you dare 'Joshie' me," Yehoshua warns, though his tone is playful. He bends his knees and lowers his head. The boy squeals before ruffling Yehoshua's hair. Hard. He messes the whole thing up. Yehoshua grabs him around the waist and flips him over his shoulder.

"I'm gonna throw up!" the boy cries.

"What's my name?" Yehoshua demands.

"Uncle Josh. Now put me down!"

Yehoshua complies. Then he catches sight of me. Surprise crawls onto his face. He lightly smacks his nephew's behind. "Go to Daddy before he thinks you got lost again."

"Okay!" The boy runs back into the hall.

Oh no. Yehoshua is heading my way. I tuck some hair behind my ear. He's *moving closer*. He's right *in front* of me.

"Hey," he says.

"Hi," I croak. I rub my upper arms.

"You have a ride home?"

"Yeah. My, um, mom is picking me up."

He nods. "Okay."

Awkward silence.

"You sing really well," I say.

Again, he looks surprised. "You heard me?" It's hard to tell in the dark, but I know he's blushing.

"Yeah," I say with a light laugh. "It's kind of hard to shut off my ears."

A small smile makes its way to his mouth. It appears as though his blush grows stronger.

"You really do have an amazing voice," I say.

"Thanks."

Another awkward silence.

His gaze seems to grow more intense. "You're not wearing your glasses."

My hand automatically goes to my nose to push my glasses

up, but of course I just feel skin. "Oh. I'm wearing contacts," I tell him. "My mom kind of forces me to wear them to such occasions."

He looks confused.

"In case there are vultures around."

His eyebrows shoot up. "Vultures?"

I laugh awkwardly. "You know. Matchmakers. Mothers of potential boys. Like maybe they'll see my exquisite beauty and snatch me before someone else does. That sort of thing."

He just stares at me. Then he bursts out laughing. "Vultures. Good one. I like it. You're funny."

My cheeks steam. "I am? I mean, thanks."

He inclines his head.

Silence yet again. I'm kind of shaking because I'm so nervous talking to him like this. I hope he can't tell.

"I like your glasses," he says.

"W…what? I mean, I like them, too. But the vultures…"

He chuckles. "Yeah. You need to look your finest."

I nod. He gets it.

Again silence.

"You sing well," I say. "Oh. I already said that."

His smile is very warm. "That's okay. It's nice hearing you

say it again."

"Is that your true passion?"

He blinks. "What?"

"You asked me yesterday if programming games is my true passion. Is singing yours?"

Darkness passes over his face.

A loud honk causes me to jump. I look toward the street and see Mom's car. "My mom's here," I tell him.

"Good night," he says. "And thanks for joining my family in our *simcha*."

"You're welcome. Good night."

I make my way to the car. Then I turn back to look at him. He's watching me. I turn back to the car and knock right into it.

Mom lowers the passenger side window. "Adina, are you okay?"

"I'm fine." I open the door and get in. As she steps on the gas, I look out the window and see Yehoshua is still watching. I keep my eyes on him until I can't see him anymore.

Chapter Ten

In honor of Mr. Markus's daughter's wedding, we don't have to come in for work the next day.

I sleep until late and work on my game. I can't stop the memories of last night from floating around in my head. Yehoshua Markus...Josh Markus. I like the name Josh. Yehoshua is so formal. Josh is playful. Fun. But of course I can't call him that.

I remember the way he looked at me and laughed at my lame jokes. Not that many people think I'm funny, especially guys. I guess it takes a certain kind of person to like my sense of humor. Yehoshua seems like one of those people.

Shaking my head, I tell myself not to grow too obsessed. I tend to do that when someone shows interest in me. Just because we had a conversation last night that was not work-related, it doesn't mean anything. And besides, he's difficult.

But I really shouldn't listen to gossip. Maybe Yehoshua is just misunderstood.

I shake my head again. I don't want to obsess like this.

My phone rings at 4 PM. It's my sister Henny. "Hey," she says. "Mom mentioned you're off from work today. Can you do me a huge favor and go out with me and the kids? I don't know what's with them today, but they are getting so cranky being cooped up in the house. If I don't get out of here, I think my head will explode."

Tehila and Akiva have finished school for today. It would be nice to hang out with them. Not to mention take my mind off Yehoshua.

"Sure," I tell her.

After getting dressed, I snack on fruit until Henny picks me up. I give Tehila, Akiva, and baby Penina a big kiss before climbing into the passenger seat. "Thanks," my sister says as she pulls out of the driveway. "I was really about to lose it." She looks at the rear-view mirror. "Akiva, don't kick your sister." She sighs and shakes her head. "Being a mother is tough," she whispers, "but I wouldn't give it up for anything."

I lean my head against the window. "So where are we

going?"

"Anywhere."

"Do you want to go shopping for some clothes?"

She glances at me, her forehead raised in surprise. "Yeah. That would be great."

Maybe she's right and I do need to buy a new wardrobe. I mean, I don't want to be stubborn and ruin my chances of getting married just because I refuse to buy new clothes. Yehoshua's face pops in front of me. A little voice in my head tells me he wouldn't care what I wear. I tell that voice to keep quiet. It doesn't matter what he thinks. And anyway, maybe he does care what girls wear. I was dressed up last night, after all, and he noticed me.

"You're always in your own world," Henny says. "Are you thinking about the game you're working on?"

I shake my head. "No. I just have too much on my mind."

She releases a breath. "Don't we all."

It's quiet, save for the kids fighting in the backseat, arguing who can draw a better picture.

Henny glances at me again. "Adina, I'm sorry if I come off too harsh sometimes. I just...it hurts me to see you so unhappy."

"I'm not unhappy."

"But you're not happy, either."

"My happiness isn't dependent on whether or not I'm married," I mutter. "I wish people would stop treating singles as though we're defected until we finally have the merit to get married."

"I'm sorry," she says. "I just know you want to get married very badly."

"I don't. I just wish I could meet the right guy already. If there even is a guy out there for me." Yehoshua's face pops into my head again. I shove it away.

"There is," Henny assures me. "Just have faith. And pray a lot."

I nod.

We finally pull up to the mall and park in the lot. Henny takes Akiva out of his car seat while I take Tehila. I balance her on my hip and kiss her cheek. Then Henny gets the stroller out of the trunk and straps the baby in. We first go to the baby and kids' section to pick out clothes for the little ones. We find the cutest outfits. Then we head downstairs for the women's department.

I puff out some air when I come face to face with the rows

of clothes. They seem to go on for miles and it's so daunting. Henny chuckles lightly when she sees the expression on my face. "Don't worry. I'm here to keep you sane."

She grabs a cart and starts loading different articles of clothing inside. They don't seem to be my style, but I don't say anything. Maybe I'll look good in them. Maybe it's time I stop being stubborn.

Henny and I talk about life and our family. Two of my brothers live in Israel and the other in England. We don't see each other a lot, and I miss them terribly.

Then it's time to try on the clothes. I choose a tight tan skirt that reaches just below my knees. It's not exactly my type because I like long skirts with cool patterns and designs on them. But I try it on, anyway. The shirt is also out of my comfort zone, but I'm willing to give it a try.

I check myself in the mirror. A girl I don't recognize stares back at me. I study myself for a few minutes before shaking my head. Even if I do look better in this, it's not me. I don't want to have to change anything just so I could get past a second date. He should accept me for who I am. As long as I look put together, I shouldn't have to worry about my outfits. It's not my clothes that are obstructing my chances at meeting the right guy. It's me.

Yehoshua didn't seem put off by me. I slam my palm on my forehead. Enough. I have to stop thinking about him.

I unlock the door to my dressing room and step out. Henny is sitting on one of the chairs outside, balancing both Akiva and Tehila on her knees and rocking the stroller. As soon as she lays her eyes on me, her whole face lights up. "Adina, you look *amazing*!"

Feeling too self-conscious, I cross my arms. "I don't know."

"C'mon, tell me you don't think you look good. You don't look like a teenager anymore but your age."

Sighing, I turn to face her. "Guys don't care what a girl wears."

"Of course they do! They might not understand what's in style or what goes well together, but they know when a girl looks attractive."

My hands move on their own to the hem of my skirt and tug on it. The skirt is modest, but I'm not accustomed to wearing such short ones. The ones I wear always touch my shoes.

"I shouldn't have to change myself," I say.

"You're not. But a person needs to grow up." She looks at her kids. "Doesn't Aunt Adina look pretty?" she asks.

"Yes!" Tehila says, pumping her fists in the air.

"I'm bored," Akiva complains.

"We'll go for pizza later," I promise. "Aunt Adina's treat."

"Yay!" they both say.

Henny wrinkles her nose. "You're going to make my kids grow up eating junk."

"Please," I tell her, tugging on the skirt again. "Pizza once in a blue moon won't kill them."

Henny struggled with her weight in high school and her early twenties. She worked really hard to lose the pounds, and when she finally succeeded, she got engaged. She's positive Dov proposed because she was thin, but I doubt that. Dov saw her for the person she is. Maybe that's why she's so concerned with how I look.

I don't want to think she may be right.

"Well, you can certainly gain some weight," Henny says. "You're skinnier than a lamppost."

"At least you were born with the personality," I mutter. "And the looks."

"Adina, you are *very* pretty. And you've got a great

personality."

"I'm sorry. I don't mean to be so insecure. All this dating drama is making me doubt everything about myself."

"New clothes might help," Henny says with a wide grin.

I roll my eyes.

"Just two outfits, Adina. You don't have to wear them throughout the week. Just on dates."

"This goes against everything I believe in," I tell her. "One shouldn't have to change in order to get married."

"Sometimes you need to do things you don't like to get what you want. You can go back to your outfits once you're married."

"That's ridiculous."

"That's life."

"Fine," I surrender. "Two outfits. Then I don't want to hear a single word."

I wait with the kids while Henny tries on some clothes. She's definitely trying to force her style on me. She's always impeccably dressed, but she's not me. We may share blood, but we are nothing alike.

Before we head back to the car, we go for a stroll in the small park near the mall. After a few minutes, Henny clutches her lower back and winces. I grab hold of her arm. "Are you okay?"

"Yeah, it's just my back."

I take hold of the stroller with one hand and use the other one to lead her to a bench. I tell the kids to stay close. As Henny sits down, she bursts into tears. I just sit there, stunned. My sister hardly ever cries. "What's wrong?"

She shakes her head and wipes her eyes. "It's nothing. I'm just being silly."

"People don't cry for no reason."

"I strained my back last night while doing the laundry."

I just look at her, confused. That's why she's crying?

"I don't think Dov is happily married to me."

I gape at her. "What? Where's this coming from?"

"That's why I hurt my back. I tripped on one of Akiva's toys. That started the argument between Dov and me last night. But it was different this time. The way he spoke to me…it wasn't like him."

I have no idea what to say. I put my arm around her shoulder, careful not to hurt her.

"I don't think he loves me anymore."

"He does, Henny. I saw the way he looked at you when you

came over for Shabbos. The same way he did at your wedding."

She rummages in her bag for a tissue. "Really?"

"Yeah. Maybe he's just stressed because of his new job. Isn't he working more hours now?"

She nods. "He hopes things will slow down soon. I'm just so worried my marriage is failing."

I take her in my arms. "Talk to him. Isn't communication the key to a successful marriage?"

She sniffs and pulls back. "Yeah. But just as a side note, communicating with your spouse isn't always easy. Lately, Dov just wants to relax when he comes home instead of discussing important matters."

"Dov is one of the kindest guys I know. I'm positive he wants to hear how you're feeling."

She nods and wipes her eyes. I try to blot out the worried thoughts flowing through my head. I've always thought Henny and Dov's marriage was perfect, one I wished to have when I meet the right guy. They're the kind of couple who are just made for each other. But what if I'm wrong and Dov isn't happy? Does that mean he'll leave Henny and the kids?

Does that mean every marriage is doomed?

Chapter Eleven

Miriam is already at the office when I walk in the next morning, hanging her jacket in the closet. She waves and wishes me a good morning. Then her eyes move over my hair. "Back to wavy? I love the straight hair."

"Yeah, I like it, too. If only it wasn't such a bother to get it straightened."

"How long does it take?" she asks as we head to our desks. "You use a hair iron?"

"Yeah. It takes like two hours."

Her eyes widen. "Wow."

"When I get married, I'll have a wig with straight hair."

"You'll miss your hair," she tells me. "Believe me."

"I believe you one hundred percent." I open my drawer and take out Greene's documents. "Is Mr. Markus going to come in today?"

"Probably. He can't afford to miss too many days."

That means Yehoshua will most likely come in. I swallow the lump that's lodged in my throat. Then I tell myself to relax because I'm pretty sure things will go back to how they used to be, with Yehoshua only talking to me about work-related things.

"You should have stayed another ten minutes at the wedding," Miriam says, her eyes laughing. "Michal and Naomi bumped into a waiter who was carrying in dessert. The ice cream fell all over the poor man's uniform. But it was so funny."

I feel a pang in my stomach. I do feel like I missed out. But I was feeling ignored at the wedding. I just wish I would break into the group already.

The other girls start to arrive, and they're still talking about the wedding. My phone rings. It's Mom. "Hi," I say.

"Hi, sweetie. Are you busy?"

"No."

"Okay. Mrs. Shain suggested you change your references on your profile."

"What? Why?"

That Special Someone

"She sent your profile to quite a few guys and hasn't heard back from any. She's worried your references may not be painting you in the best light."

"But I have my favorite high school teacher listed, Avigayil, and Aunt Judy."

"I know. Maybe you should add another teacher? Maybe one of your old coworkers? Or your new ones."

I glance around and notice all the girls' ears are perked. I go to the conference room and close the door. "Mom, that's ridiculous. My references are painting me in the best light possible. Did...did it ever occur to you that maybe people are saying no because...because..." I swallow the rest of the sentence. *Because of Dad?* I can't bear to say it.

Mom knows exactly what I'm talking about. "I married off four kids without *that* affecting anything," she says.

"So I'm just a bad seed."

"No, Adina—"

"I really appreciate all you're doing for me, Mom. Really. But if the guys Mrs. Shain is reaching out to think they're too good for me, then maybe she needs to find better guys."

"Adina—"

"My boss just walked in," I lie. "We'll talk at home, okay?"

"Okay. I love you, Adina."

"Love you, too."

I sit down at my desk, huffing and puffing. Why is it so hard to meet a decent guy? I wish I could look into a crystal ball and see who I'm destined to marry.

One good thing about work is that I can focus all my energy on it and forget about dating. Mr. Greene's documents are so frustrating, though. They make me want to pull my hair out.

The front door opens and Yehoshua steps in. I freeze, my pen raised in the air. He's dressed in a black jacket with a dark blue shirt peeking from underneath, and dark pants. Unlike at the wedding, his hair is disheveled. His yarmulke manages to sit neatly on his head without sliding off.

When our eyes meet, I feel like the air gets knocked out of me. He gives me a warm smile. I feel my cheeks rise. He says, "Good morning," to everyone before walking into his office.

My pen is still raised in the air. I quickly lower it and continue working.

A few minutes later, Mr. Markus walks inside.

"*Mazel tov*, Mr. Markus," Shaindy says. "The wedding was beautiful."

That Special Someone

"And your daughter looked gorgeous," Michal says.

"*Mazel tov, mazel tov,*" he says, a huge grin on his face. "The joy a parent feels when he marries off one of his children." His eyes narrow at Yehoshua's closed door. "Now, if I could just get rid of that one, my life would be much easier."

We all laugh, but mine is cut short. What exactly does he mean by that? Is Yehoshua having a hard time dating? How old is he, anyway? He doesn't look more than twenty-seven. But I shouldn't be delving so deeply into this.

Mr. Markus stops by my desk. "Did you and Yehoshua start working on Greene?"

"Yeah. I'm trying to get his papers in order."

"Good. I just wanted to make sure Yehoshua isn't getting lazy." He winks. "If you have any problems, speak to him. I really would like him to try to take this on his own without my guidance. I'm sure you will be a tremendous help to him."

I nod.

He enters his son's office. "Yehoshua! Look at that. You're here before me...." I don't hear what else they're saying because the door shuts.

I focus on my work. After a little while, Mr. Markus leaves his son's office. Needing to stretch my legs, I head over to the bin that holds all the papers that need to be filed. A lot has piled up, since I haven't filed in a few days.

It feels nice to be alone in the conference room. As much as I don't want to think about dating, I feel relaxed and in peace when I file. And since I'm in privacy, I can hum to myself. I'm a terrible singer, but I sometimes like to hum when I work. It helps the time pass.

I get down on my knees and search through the files in the back of the bottom drawer. It's so annoying when they're all falling over each other and are hard to access. "Get over here, you file," I start to sing. "Adina wants to add a paper to the pile." I giggle. "Filing is fun, it relaxes my mind. Makes me think of thoughts that are pleasant and kind—"

"Hey, is someone in here?"

My mouth snaps shut. Yehoshua! Did he hear me singing?

I get up so fast I bang my head into one of the folders sitting on the shelf against the wall. It falls on me before crashing to the floor.

"Sorry I scared you," he says, stepping in. "Are you okay?"

Some of the papers are stuck to my hair because of the paperclips and staples. I pull them off, but one of them is stuck. "Ow," I say when I yank on it again. The staple is caught.

"Here, let me," he says, stepping even closer. I find myself pressed against the wall as Yehoshua reaches for my hair. He hesitates for a second before gently freeing the paper, then he steps back. "Sorry about that." He bends to retrieve the folder and loose papers.

He *touched* my hair.

"Thanks," I say, my voice trembling.

He stands and puts the papers in the folder. "No problem."

We just look at each other.

I rub the area on my scalp that stings a little due to the staple that was caught. "D-did you want something?" I ask, my voice still shaky.

"Oh yeah. Sorry. I was looking for you. Did you have a chance to get Greene's papers in order?"

"Yeah. But there are some things I'm confused about, and he has so many payments on his bank statements and credit cards…"

"Okay. Do you want to meet in my office and discuss them?"

"Okay."

"Whenever you're ready. Just stop by my office."

I nod.

He gives me a small nod before leaving. Oh my gosh. He *touched* my hair.

I'm not in the right state to go back to my desk. Even though I've filed the last paper, I stay seated on the floor near the bottom drawer and just think. After a few minutes, I force myself to get up and return to my desk. I'm almost done with Greene's papers, I just need to type a few more things into the program. I move at a snail's pace because I'm too nervous to meet with Yehoshua. He heard me singing. He *touched* my hair.

But what can I do? Avoid him for the rest of my life?

When I'm done, I print out whatever I need and hold them in my hands. I sit at my desk for a few minutes, telling myself to relax, before getting up and walking toward Yehoshua's office. *Whatever you do*, I tell myself, *please don't make a fool of yourself.*

I close my hand over the knob and pull the door open. Yehoshua's elbows are resting on his desk and his hands are pressed to his temples. He seems to be reading something very intently. He must not have heard me come in. I take a few steps closer.

His head jerks up. "Ready?" he asks, slipping the paper into his desk drawer.

"Yeah."

He motions for me to sit down. Once I do, his eyes land on the pile of papers I'm holding. "All of that?" he asks.

I nod.

He whistles. "This is not going to be fun. Okay, what have we got?"

I clear my throat. "One of the companies he owns—the one that gives him the most profit—is a bakery." I start telling him about Mr. Greene's other businesses. Then I show him his bank statements and credit cards. "I don't understand what the payments are for. I guess I'll have to call him."

"Okay, Adina."

My throat gets dry. This is the first time he's said my name. It sounds very…sweet coming from him.

I clear my throat again. "I'm going to need help figuring out the depreciation on some of his things," I say, looking through the papers. "And I'm not very clear on the tax due dates on all of his companies. Also, he had a major loss on one of his businesses last year—"

"Why programming?" he asks.

"What?"

"I doubt I can find many girls your age spending their free

time coding on their computers. So why?"

His question catches me off guard. Not many people want to know what got me into programming. They just want to know why I do it in the first place. "Oh, um…I was alone a lot as a kid—" I stop myself before I pour out my whole life story, how after my dad walked out on us, I used to stay home and only leave the house for school. Kids thought I was weird. They didn't understand what I was going through. "I was once at the library," I continue. "My mom told me to find a good novel to read, but I found a book on programming instead. I thought it was cool. It had a disc in the back. I checked it out of the library and tried the disc. I was hooked. I begged my mom to buy me my own copy of the software and spent the next few days devouring the book. Then I spent the next few weeks trying to learn to code." I laugh sheepishly. "I thought it was the coolest thing in the world."

He's looking at me with fascination, like I just told him the secret to how to make a million bucks in five minutes.

I tuck some hair behind my ear. "A few years ago, I started working on my first game for the mobile phone."

"Is that the same one you're working on now?"

I nod.

That Special Someone

"Can I please see it?" he asks, real intrigue in his eyes.

"I don't like showing it to anyone until it's finished."

"Who have you shown it to?"

I lower my gaze to his desk. "No one. I mean, no one has seemed that interested. Other than my mom." But lately, she hasn't shown much support, since she's so worried about my single status.

"Can I be the first person you show it to?" he asks, his voice soft.

I slowly lift my eyes to his. "I don't know."

"Please. I'm sure it's amazing. I won't tell anyone. I promise."

He's giving me the puppy dog look, pouting his lips. I can't help but laugh. "Are you really that interested? It's so close to my heart."

"I really am. I think what you do is so cool. Actually, it's cooler than cool."

I find myself laughing again.

The truth is, I'm dying to show my game to someone, someone special. I always assumed it would be the person I'd marry. But Yehoshua looks genuinely interested. That makes me feel really good.

"Are you sure?" I ask. "I mean, shouldn't we…?" My gaze falls to the papers on his desk.

"It's okay," he says. "We'll get back to work right after."

I return to my desk. All the girls look up from what they're doing, their expressions curious. I dig in my bag for my phone and make my way back to Yehoshua's office, sliding into my chair. My fingers are shaking as I unlock my phone and scroll to the game. "You have to promise to be honest."

"I promise." He gets up and sits down near me on the second chair in front of his desk. I freeze. He's *sitting* near me.

I blink. "Um, here." I hold out my phone that's loading the game. "You have to—"

"No, please don't tell me. I want to figure it out by myself. I love doing that. I never read instructions on how to play games."

I laugh lightly. "Mine doesn't have instructions yet. It doesn't even have a second level."

He laughs, too. "Can I take it?"

I nod.

Even though he takes my phone, he bends close so that I can see the screen. He's sitting so close to me. It causes my heart rate to pick up.

That Special Someone

"This is so cute," he says as the on-screen dialogue plays. "A little girl falls off a tree and passes out. She wakes up in a magical land."

"Well, she's not supposed to be that young," I say, pushing up my glasses that are sliding down my nose. "She should be a teenager. I guess I need to work harder on my artwork."

"No, it's perfect. I love it."

He said he loves it. That's makes me feel really good, that all my hard work is actually paying off.

"So I need to move her," he says, his thumbs tapping on the screen. The girl keeps walking until she falls into some water. She transforms into a fish. Yehoshua's face lights up. "So cool! My nieces and nephews would love this. I love it. I bet people of all ages would love it, too."

He raises his head and our eyes lock. I sit back. We're too close.

He coughs before focusing his attention back on the game. After a few seconds, he smiles. "And when I jump high in the air, I turn into a bird. This is so much fun."

"Thanks," I say, both embarrassed and elated. He's the first person I've shown my game to. I don't know how I feel exactly. Exposed, vulnerable. But proud, too.

When he finishes the level, which involves fighting the boss that is a huge fish, the biggest frown I've ever seen on a person overtakes his face. "It's over?" he asks.

"That's all I have so far."

He puts my phone down on the desk. "It's such a good game, Adina."

"Thanks…Yehoshua."

He gives me a very warm smile.

"It makes me feel really good that you like it."

"You should feel good," he says. "You're so talented."

"Thanks." I'm about to tell him that he's talented, too, but then I remember the dark look on his face when I mentioned his singing at the wedding.

He returns to his chair and leans back. I assume he's going to focus his attention on Mr. Greene's documents, but he says, "So what else do you like to do?"

"I like to read."

"Me too. What kind of books?"

"Mysteries and thrillers."

"Cool. What other genres do you like?"

"Well, I enjoy a good, clean romance novel as much as the next girl. But lately, it's been hard to enjoy them. They all end with happily ever afters and…" I don't want to finish my sentence.

"How old are you?" he asks.

"Twenty-Five. You?"

"Twenty-Six. I thought you were younger. You look very young."

"My sister thinks it's because I still dress like a teenager."

"What?"

Oh my gosh, did I say that out loud? "Um, nothing."

"No, what?" he asks his eyes lit with curiosity.

"Are you sure you want to talk about women's clothes?" I ask.

"Sure. Everything you've said so far has been interesting."

My heart rate starts to spike. Is he really that interested? He has to be, because one thing I learned about guys is if they're interested, they will talk to you. If Yehoshua found me boring, he would just discuss Mr. Greene.

"I like these kinds of skirts," I say, pointing to my skirt. It's light blue with dark blue designs on them. Yehoshua stands to take a look. "My sister thinks I don't dress my age," I tell him. "She thinks I need to change my style."

"I don't think you should listen to your sister. I like your style. Not that it matters what I think."

Oh, it matters. It matters a lot.

"Why are we talking about my clothes?" I say with a nervous laugh.

"You're the one who brought it up."

"I know. I'm sorry."

He waves his hand. "Don't be. But we should probably get back to work."

"Yeah," I say reluctantly. Talking to him is fun. I don't think I've ever enjoyed talking to a guy as much as I'm enjoying talking to Yehoshua Markus. That's probably because we're not on a date. There's no pressure.

But could it be something more than that?

Chapter Twelve

As soon as I walk into the house, Mom bounces over. "A guy is interested!"

"What?" I don't want to hear about potential guys. I just want to think about Yehoshua like I've been doing ever since I left his office after we worked on Mr. Greene's documents.

I head to the fridge and poke around in it.

"Now this one comes from a very good family—"

"Mom, I think I want to take a break."

"No. Absolutely not. Once you take a break, it's hard to get back out there."

I close my eyes before pulling away from the fridge and facing her. "Do you realize that all this dating drama is taking over my life? All everyone ever does is talk about me and boys. You and I don't even *talk* anymore."

"Adina, don't blow things out of proportion. We talk plenty. But right now, you need to focus on dating. Not programming and all those other nonsense."

It feels like she took one of the kitchen knives and stabbed me in the heart. "Did you just call my programming 'nonsense?'"

Her face falls. "I didn't mean—"

"I don't even know who you are anymore," I say, tears entering my eyes. "You've turned into one of those mothers who obsess over her daughter getting married. That's not you. It's never been you."

Her mouth closes. She just stares at me, a hurt look on her face.

I feel horrible for what I just said. "I'm sorry."

"I didn't think you'd be twenty-five and not married, sweetie," she says.

"Nothing's wrong with being twenty-five and not married!"

"Don't you understand, Adina? I am your only parent. It's my responsibility to find you a good husband who will take care of you."

"What on Earth?"

"I'm not going to live forever. Who's going to take care of

you?"

"I don't need anyone to take care of me, Mom! I don't need a man to make me happy."

She sighs and brings the back of her fingers to her forehead. "You've been reading too many books."

"No, I haven't."

She touches her heart. "Do you have any idea how much it hurts me? To see the defeated and pained look on your face when you come back from a failed date? Do you know how much it *hurts* me?"

I don't say anything.

"You were crushed when your father left," she says, tears starting to slide down her cheeks. "I was the one who held you in my arms and wiped your tears. I was the one who took care of you."

My vision is blurry due to the tears that are gushing down my cheeks. Mom hardly ever mentions my father.

"Every time you're hurting, I feel it deep in here." She jabs her chest. "Every time you cry, I cry, too."

I gather her in my arms and hug her tight. I don't need to say anything. It's enough that I just hold her. Mom breaks down on me. I rub her back.

After her sobs have died down, I say, "Everything will be okay. God willing, I'll find a husband. Hashem will send him to me when I'm ready. When the time is right."

"I'm so sorry, Adina. I didn't mean to blow up on you. I just want to see you happy. That's all I want."

"I know. And I want to make you happy, too. I don't want you to worry about me."

She pulls away and holds me at arm's length. "There's nothing you can do about that. A mother always worries about her kids. Even when they're all grown up."

"I'll make you some tea," I offer.

"Thanks, sweetie."

I make tea for both Mom and me, and we sit at the table and just talk. About everything, about nothing. I wasn't exaggerating when I told my mother we hardly talk. It's like a dam burst open and we can't stop talking.

"If you feel you need to take a break, I'm okay with it," Mom tells me. "But only a short one. I don't want Mrs. Shain to give up on you."

"Thanks for understanding."

I help her with dinner and once we're done eating and cleaning up, I go up to my room to work on my game.

That Special Someone

Yehoshua's excitement for it has lit a fire inside me. If he likes it, maybe others can, too. Maybe I can finally get it out there and fulfil my dream.

***

Ugh, it's one of *those* days. No matter what I do, I can't seem to tame my hair. It usually behaves itself every morning, despite being frizzy, but I don't think I can win the battle this time. Maybe my lack of sleep has contributed to this. I couldn't stop thinking about Yehoshua.

I wonder if he thinks about me. Or if he sees me as nothing more than his coworker who happens to program games, which he happens to enjoy. Maybe, like usual, I'm thinking too deeply into this.

But the prospect of working with him again makes every cell in my body dance. I don't think I've ever felt this excited about a guy before.

I spend a little longer than usual getting ready, choosing an outfit carefully. I wish I didn't care about outside appearances, but I do want to look good in front of Yehoshua. I make sure my socks have no holes, that my shoes are matched, and that my shirt has no stains. I check my reflection in the mirror twice before heading downstairs for breakfast. Mom has already left.

I munch on some cake and down a glass of orange juice. Then I make my way to the bus stop. Today is colder than yesterday. I pull my jacket closer to my body and bounce in my place. Finally, the bus pulls up. I take my usual seat in the back.

When it reaches my stop, I get off and walk to the office. The door is unlocked, which means someone is already in. But the lights are shut. I hope Mr. Markus didn't forget to lock up last night. As I'm hanging up my jacket, I hear movement behind me and I spin around. Something cold and bubbly splashes my face, burning my eyes. It drips down my face and I taste it—Coke.

"Adina! I'm sorry."

Even though my eyes sting from the liquid, my body stiffens. Yehoshua.

"I'll get you a paper towel," he says before I hear him hurry to the bathroom. I wipe my sleeve across my eyes.

Yehoshua returns with a mountain of paper towels. He hands them to me. "Thanks," I say and wipe my face. I'm all sticky.

"Sorry," he says again. "I was about to wish you a good morning when you turned around and knocked my cup of Coke out of my hand."

That Special Someone

"It's okay," I say, trying to muster a smile. I'm embarrassed. Really embarrassed. Why do these things *have* to happen in front of him?

I walk into the bathroom and splash water on my face. When I see myself in the mirror, I try not to groan. My hair is a mess. It was a mess before this incident, but now it looks like a hurricane swept through it. I try to pat it down in place, but the strands seem to have the ability to defy gravity.

When I leave the bathroom, Yehoshua is still in the kitchen. "Are you okay?" he asks.

"Yeah."

"I ruined your hair."

I pat it down again. "No, you're not to blame for this monstrosity. I woke up to it." I pat it again.

"Oh. Okay," he says with a relieved laugh. "I know some girls take hours to work on their hair. I was worried I messed it up."

"It—it's okay. I don't really care about my hair. I mean, of course I care, I just don't freak out about it all the time. If I would, I would be totally gray by now." I pat it for a third time.

Yehoshua laughs, his demeanor much more relaxed and less guilt-ridden. "Did I scare you? I didn't mean to."

I look around the office, which is still bathed in darkness. "The lights were off, so I didn't know anyone else was in here."

He rubs the back of his neck. "Oh. I like to work in the dark sometimes."

"You do? I do, too!" I don't mean to sound overly excited by the fact that he and I have something in common. But I am.

His face washes with surprise. "You do, too? My mom's always on my case about it. She says I'm ruining my eyes."

I laugh. "Mine says the same thing."

He smiles. I smile.

Awkward silence.

He shifts in his place. I hug my upper arms.

"I worked on my game last night," I find myself saying.

His face lights up. "You did? Did I inspire you?"

I blush. How does he know he's the reason I worked on the game for four hours straight last night?

"You can't ask me that," I say, my voice wobbly.

"Why not?"

"Because if I say yes, you'll get cocky and demand fifty percent of my profit."

"I promise I will never take any of your profits. Even if you put me in as one of the playable characters."

That Special Someone

"Okay." I don't know what else to say.

Awkward silence again.

"I should probably pour myself another cup of Coke," he says, walking to the fridge.

"I'm sorry I knocked it out of your hand."

"Don't worry about it." He pulls out the Coke bottle.

"It just kind of happens to me. I don't mean to do it on purpose."

"You don't have to make excuses for being who you are," he says.

He's right. But I don't want him to be put off by me. I also don't want him to think I'm insecure. "I'll, um, get to work."

"On Greene?" he asks.

I nod.

"I need to work on something for my dad this morning. But you're welcome to come see me if you need to."

"Okay."

He twists open the cap of the Coke bottle. "Would you like a drink?"

Of course my mouth gets parched at the mention of it. "Yes, thanks."

He hands me the cup. His finger accidentally brushes

against mine. A strange feeling passes through me. I nearly drop the cup.

"Sorry," he says.

"It's okay." I head for my desk before I do another clumsy thing. Yehoshua is still standing by the kitchen. There's a large mirror hanging on the door of the closet. He can see me and I can see him. Our eyes lock on one another for a few seconds before I look away.

He goes to his office.

The door opens and Miriam walks in, followed by Shaindy and Michal. They're in the middle of a conversation. I can't help feeling left out when I see how friendly they are with one another. My thoughts drift to Yehoshua. We're not...friends, are we? I mean, men and women are not supposed to be friends in my community. But Yehoshua and I kind of are. I've shared something with him yesterday.

But this is useless. After we're done with Mr. Greene's taxes, we probably won't talk again. I mean, of course we'll exchange a few words with each other since we're coworkers, but we won't *talk*.

"Hey," Miriam says, rolling over to me. "I want to tell you something. But you have to promise not to tell anyone.

Especially the girls here."

"Okay. I might be a bit clumsy, but thank God my mouth isn't. Your secret is safe with me."

She leans forward and whispers, "I'm pregnant!"

I fling my arms around her. "That's awesome!"

Michal and Faigy look our way, their foreheads wrinkled.

"*Mazel tov*," I whisper to her.

"I just found out yesterday. I had to tell someone other than my husband. If I tell any of my other friends, they'll tell the whole world. I kind of want to keep it a secret for now."

"I'm so excited for you."

"Thanks." She hugs me, squeezing me really tight.

"Can't breathe," I rasp.

She loosens her hold. "Sorry. I'm just so excited."

"I can totally see you as a mommy," I say. "You'll be amazing."

Her cheeks darken. "You think so?"

"I know so."

"Thanks. Hey, did you look into the guy whose profile I emailed you?"

"Yeah. I don't think he's right for me. Thanks, though."

Yehoshua walks out of his office and stops before my desk.

"I need to go out. I don't know how long it'll take. Is it okay if I give you my number in case you have any questions?"

"Yes."

I hand him a piece of paper and he scribbles it down. "If my dad comes in, can you tell him I went over to Kalman Segal?"

"Sure."

"Thanks."

He leaves the office.

"How's working with him?" Miriam asks.

"It's good. He told me Mr. Markus wants him to do Mr. Greene's taxes all on his own without his guidance."

Miriam looks surprised. "That's interesting. I wonder if he's going to give him a managerial role."

"How long has he been working here?"

"He's been working here on and off for the past five years. This time, I think he's been here for a little over a year. Right, Michal?"

She looks over her shoulder and thinks. "I think so. He came back last summer."

"Oh. So he doesn't stay for long." I don't know why that makes me feel a little dejected.

That Special Someone

"Faigy wants to take bets," Michal says.

"But that's mean," Shaindy says.

"I wish I had the luxury of coming and going when I please," Naomi mutters.

The front door opens and Mr. Markus walks in. We all turn our attention to our work.

"Good morning, good morning," he half-sings as he moves deeper into the office. "Yehoshua?" He opens his son's office door. "Did Yehoshua come in yet?"

I'm about to answer when Naomi pipes up. "Yes, he did, but he left to see Kalman Segal. He's not sure when he'll be back, but he made sure to leave a message with *me*, so that you'll know." She juts out her chin, her eyes pasted on mine.

She *wishes* Yehoshua left the message with her. I don't even understand why she's behaving this way. It's not like Yehoshua and I are...anything. I'm the one sitting at the front desk and he's *supposed* to leave messages with me.

"Why didn't he call me?" Mr. Markus slips his hand into his pocket and takes out his phone. "Dead again? Why did that boy insist he buy me a smartphone? It's making me more dumb than smart!"

The six of us try not to laugh.

He nods to Naomi. "Thanks for letting me know."

"No problem, Mr. Markus." If her grin was any wider, she'd have no face left. I think she's trying to make a good impression on Mr. Markus. Maybe she hopes he'd be taken away by her and will tell his son to go out with her.

I wish they would go on a date so she'd leave me alone. Actually, no. I don't want him to go out with her. I want him to go out with me.

I gasp when I realize what thoughts are spinning in my mind.

"What?" Miriam asks, eyes alarmed. "Did you see a cockroach?" She frantically looks at the floor.

"No, sorry! I just…never mind."

"As long as it's not a cockroach. I'm telling you, I don't know why Hashem created those creatures, but they are a major contributing factor to my bug phobia."

"I think almost every girl has a bug phobia," I tell her.

"Not like me." She yanks open her bottom drawer, and I see three bottles of bug spray.

I try not to laugh. "At least you're prepared."

I've started a list of questions I need to ask Mr. Greene. There are too many. I look over his documents for the millionth time, making sure I don't miss anything because I'd like to ask him my questions all at once. But something catches my attention. I'm not sure if it's a mistake or if I don't understand what I'm looking at. I gnaw on my bottom lip as my gaze treks to the piece of paper with Yehoshua's number. I don't want to call him. I'd feel awkward and embarrassed. But I really do want to speak to Mr. Greene. I decide to text Yehoshua.

After I compose the message, I read it over twice to make sure it reads well, then send it. I wring my hands in my lap as I wait for his response. What if he's upset I texted him? He did give me his number, though. But what if he just did that because he was supposed to?

I tell my mind to be quiet.

I jump in my seat when my phone rings. A number I don't recognize flashes on the screen. Wait, I do recognize it—it's the one I just texted.

With a shaky hand, I answer. "Hello?"

"Hey, it's Yehoshua. I can't text now because I'm walking. What's your question?"

He sounds so different on the phone. His voice is deep and masculine.

"Adina? You there?"

I snap out of it and ask him my question. After he answers it, I say, "Thank you."

"You're welcome. Did my dad come in?"

"Yes, he's here."

"You gave him my message?"

"Yeah, he got it."

"I called, but he never answers his phone."

"I think his battery died."

He's quiet for a few seconds. "That would explain a lot."

"I think he's struggling with his new smartphone." My tone holds a tint of laughter.

Yehoshua chuckles. "Yeah. I guess that wasn't the wisest investment. So, do you have any other questions?"

"I'm good for now. I'll call Mr. Greene as soon as we hang up."

"Okay. Let me know how it goes."

We hang up and I call Mr. Greene. The conversation goes well. He's a pleasant guy and very helpful. Once all my questions are answered, I continue working on his documents.

Yehoshua doesn't return until lunchtime. He walks in when I'm in the middle of scribbling in my notebook. He stops by my desk. "You spoke to him?"

"Yeah. I'm ready to discuss."

"Okay, but I have to meet with my dad first." He makes a move to leave, then stops and looks down at my notebook. "Are you working on the game?"

Everyone in the office is staring at us. I feel my cheeks flush as I nod.

"I can't wait to play the next level." He walks into his father's office.

Naomi's eyes narrow at me. Everyone else just looks confused and curious. One by one, they go back to work. I continue with my notes.

When my lunch hour is over, I continue working. Yehoshua doesn't leave his father's office until the end of the day.

I wait a few minutes before gathering my papers and heading to his office.

Chapter Thirteen

I knock on the door before walking into Yehoshua's office. He smiles when he sees me. I sit down in one of the chairs and spread the papers out in front of me. Then I start updating him.

When I'm done, he nods. "You did a great job."

"Thanks."

Silence.

He clears his throat. "I guess we can start working on his returns."

"Okay."

I should gather the papers and leave. But I don't want to. I like being in the same room as him. "So…um…"

"Yeah?" he asks.

"You never told me what your true passion is."

That Special Someone

His gaze drops to his hands before he says, "I'm not passionate about anything like you are. I don't have the drive and determination like you do."

"What about singing?"

That same darkness passes over his face. He doesn't say anything. Why does he always get that look when his singing is mentioned?

My shoe taps on the floor. "How's um…how's your sister doing? The one who just got married."

"She's so happy it's sick," he says. He laughs lightly. "Actually, it's really nice to see her so happy. She struggled with dating."

"Really? How old is she?"

"Thirty-one."

"Oh. I thought she was younger than you."

He shakes his head. "I'm the youngest in my family."

"You are? I thought you were with your younger sister when you walked down the aisle."

"Nope. That's my niece."

"Oh. Well, we have something in common. I'm the youngest in my family, too."

He smiles.

Silence again.

"I guess I should go…" I start getting up.

"What's your favorite food?" he asks.

I sit back down. "Um…I don't know." I'm totally blanking now.

He laughs. "Everyone has a favorite food."

"Chocolate, I guess. Does that count?"

"I don't know. What real food do you like?"

"I love everything," I say. "I can't choose. What's your favorite?"

It doesn't take him more than a second to say, "Anything with potatoes. Salads, soup, stews. Anything. I love potatoes."

"Yum. I love potatoes, too."

He smiles again. And once again, it's quiet.

"I do make the most amazing potato salad," he says.

"Yum. Potato salad is delicious."

We both laugh. My leg twitches.

Someone knocks on the door. Naomi walks in. "I have a question for Adina."

"Okay," I say.

"Did you start working on Stein's Jewelry's bank statements?"

"Yeah, but I didn't have a chance to finish them. Why?"

"No, I was just wondering. Because you put in the information wrong."

My cheeks warm up. "Oh, I'm sorry."

"It's fine," Naomi says. "I'll fix it."

"Thanks for telling me."

She nods before glancing at Yehoshua and leaving.

Major awkward silence.

Yehoshua is about to say something, when the door opens and Naomi walks back in. "Can I talk to you?" She directs the question to him.

"Sure." He looks at me. "Do you have any more questions or are you good?"

"I'm good." I gather the papers and make my way to the door, passing Naomi who has a small scowl on her face. I get back to my desk and continue working.

After a few minutes, the door to Yehoshua's office opens, then I hear the door of the bathroom shut. A second or two later, Yehoshua marches out of his office and heads straight for the front door, a troubled look on his face. He shuts it firmly behind him.

I look at Miriam and she looks at me. Then we look at the

other girls. They're just as puzzled.

The bathroom door opens and Naomi walks out. She's close to tears.

"What happened?" Michal asks.

She doesn't say anything as she settles down at her desk.

Michal leaps to her feet and puts her hand on her shoulder. "What happened, Naomi?"

"I…" She hiccups. "I thought I could be confident and ask him straight out why he doesn't want to go out with me." Her lower lip trembles. "He said he thinks I'm a really nice girl, but he doesn't want to get involved with any of his coworkers."

My blood turns cold. He doesn't want to go out with anyone from work? Then…what exactly are he and I doing? Maybe he just sees me as a friend. I mean, not a friend, since he probably doesn't hang out with girls, but an acquaintance.

You don't want him to be just an acquaintance, a little voice says in my head. I shove it away.

"He wasn't a jerk at all," Naomi says, a sob in her voice. "He said it in such a nice way."

"Now you can move on," Miriam tells her. "Meet the right person who will be good to you."

"I just wish…" She sniffs. "It sucks."

That Special Someone

"He probably doesn't want to hurt you like he hurt Suri," I say. "He probably feels horrible for what happened. Maybe he doesn't want to put you through the same thing."

Naomi's eyes narrow at me.

"Adina's right," Shaindy says. "We all saw what happened when he and Suri broke up. You don't want that to happen to you, do you?"

"I guess not." She wipes her hand across her eyes. "Do you think he would go out with me if he really, *really* liked me?" she asks. "Maybe he's just using the coworker thing as an excuse?"

Miriam rolls over to her. "Listen. You shouldn't cry over him like this. You're only hurting yourself. You can meet a great guy, someone who will care deeply about you. But you'll never get there if you're still hung up on Yehoshua."

She wipes her eyes again and nods. "You're right. Ugh." She covers her face. "Why did I have to confront him? I'm so embarrassed."

"It's good you confronted him," I tell her. "Sometimes you need to stand up for yourself."

She gives me a face like I have no permission to breathe the same air as her. I shrug and focus on my work. The girls return to theirs.

Ten minutes pass before the door opens and Yehoshua strides in. He still has that troubled look on his face. He must feel really guilty for rejecting Naomi.

I try to block out the thoughts invading my mind. He clearly doesn't plan on going out with any of the girls here. That includes me. Then why does he make it seem like he's interested in me? The way he laughs at my jokes and asks about my programming. Is he just toying with my emotions?

This is giving me a headache.

When there's about an hour left to work, I realize I need help. Not wanting to bother Yehoshua, I ask the other girls if they could help, but they are just as clueless as me. I definitely don't want to bother Mr. Markus, especially because he'd like Yehoshua and me to work on Greene's returns without his guidance. I have no choice but to seek Yehoshua.

I tell myself there's no reason to be nervous around him anymore. He and I will never go out. As much as that stings a little, I have to admit I'm relieved. Now I don't have to feel uneasy whenever we're in the same room.

After knocking on his door, I peek in. "Can I ask you something?"

"Sure." He motions for me to come in.

That Special Someone

I sit in the chair and place the papers on his desk. He still has the same troubled look on his face.

He and I discuss my questions. When we're done, he says, "All clear?" He has a smile on his face, but it doesn't quite reach his eyes.

"Yes, thanks."

I get up and turn toward the door.

"Hey, Adina?"

I turn back around.

"Do you want me to help you put the information in the program? I can show you some tricks the other girls probably don't know about."

"Okay."

He gets up from his chair and motions for me to sit. He wants me to *sit* in his chair? That seems...I don't know. Like I'm invading his personal space.

I make my way there and trip over my feet, almost crashing into him. The chair breaks my fall.

Yehoshua's hands are up, like he was about to save me from uncertain death. "You okay?"

"Yeah," I say. "The floor must not like me."

That causes him to laugh.

I sit down in his chair and nearly sink into it. It's so soft. And I'm way too short—my legs dangle.

"You can adjust it," Yehoshua offers.

"It's okay."

"Okay. Log into your name."

Once I do, Yehoshua leans over me and points out what I did right and where I went wrong, though I didn't make too many mistakes. I can't help but notice how *close* he is to me. I play with my fingers on my lap.

"I'm sure in just a few weeks you'll be telling *us* how to use the program, Miss Programmer," he says, his tone fun.

I laugh awkwardly.

He prints the statements for one of Greene's companies, and we sit down to discuss it.

Someone knocks on the door and walks in. Mr. Markus. He's wearing his jacket. "How's it going?" he asks.

"Great," Yehoshua says.

"Glad to hear. I'm leaving now. Don't forget the *sheva brochos* tonight, Yehoshua."

"I won't."

Mr. Markus nods to me. "Good night, Adina."

"Good night."

That Special Someone

Once his father leaves, Yehoshua grabs his phone. "I'm totally going to forget." He punches in a reminder.

"Where is it being held?" I ask.

"At a Chinese restaurant."

"Yum. I love Chinese food."

He looks up from his phone and his whole face softens with a smile. He gazes back at his phone and continues punching things in. "So what else do you like? Other than programming, reading, and eating yummy food."

"Nothing, really. I'm boring."

"No, you're not.

"I kind of am."

"Believe me, you're not."

"You're not either," I say.

His eyebrows shoot up and he grins. "Did I say I was?"

I get all flustered.

He grins again. "I'm just teasing you. I am actually pretty boring, though."

"We can go on all day."

"We can."

We both grow silent.

Yehoshua shifts in his seat. "I started reading a great book last night. I think you'll love it." He takes out a pad of paper, scribbles something down, rips it off and holds it out to me. My hand is so shaky that it knocks right into his. The paper crashes on his desk.

The same strange sensation I felt when he handed me the cup of Coke this morning passes through me again. "Sorry!" I say.

He picks up the piece of paper and gives it to me. "No problem."

I scan what's written on it. Based on the title, it seems like a book I'll enjoy. "Thanks," I tell him. "I'll check it out."

He nods.

Quiet.

Yehoshua coughs. I feel like a fool just sitting here. I'm about to get up, but he says, "What do you parents do?"

This question always makes me uncomfortable. It forces the Dad issue to the surface. I stare down at my nails and mutter, "My mom's a nurse."

He nods. "And your dad?"

I try to square my shoulders and look as nonchalant as possible, but I know I'm failing miserably. Dad's leaving still hurts deep. "Um…" My throat closes up.

That Special Someone

Yehoshua must notice how uneasy I am because he says, "My mom owns a clothing business."

"He's not part of my life anymore," I blurt out. I don't know why I told him this—he gave me a free pass. I guess I don't want him to think something is seriously wrong with my family. Not that he wants to go out with me or anything. I should have kept quiet.

His eyes fill with sympathy. "I'm sorry to hear that."

I fight back the tears threatening to pour out of my eyes. "Thanks."

Silence yet again.

I concentrate on not blinking so the tears won't fall. I don't want to break down in front of him. He probably sees I'm fighting off tears. This is embarrassing.

Yehoshua drums his fingers on his desk. "What's your favorite Chinese food?"

I swallow a few times so that my voice won't shake before answering, "Sweet and sour chicken."

"Mine's sesame."

"I make sesame chicken."

He looks surprised. "You do?"

"Yeah. I mean, it sucks compared to the professionals."

Chaya T. Hirsch

"I'm sure it's delicious."

"Thanks. I'm sure your potato salad is delicious."

He grins. "Oh, it is."

That makes me laugh.

"You have a cute laugh," he says.

My cheeks heat up.

He shakes his head. "Sorry if I embarrassed you."

I wave my hand. "I always tell people not to apologize for embarrassing me because I do a good job at embarrassing myself."

Now he laughs. "You're so funny. But really, I'm sorry if I embarrassed you. I just think your laugh is cute."

"Thanks. Your voice is very manly. Like masculine. Especially on the phone." My eyes widen when I realize what just came out of my mouth.

He laughs again. "It's not only your laugh that's cute. You are."

My blush intensifies.

"Sorry," he says. "Sometimes I say whatever is on my mind."

"Me, too."

He laughs softly. "I know. That's what makes you cute."

That Special Someone

"Thanks."

Silence.

He shifts in his seat again. "So, Dini, did I just prove that you're not boring?"

I blink at him. "Did you just call me Dini?"

His face clouds. "Does that offend you?"

I quickly shake my head. "No, it doesn't. I mean…" I puff out some air. "My dad called me Dini."

His face clouds even more. "I am so sorry—"

"No, it's okay. I've always liked it. I kind of miss it."

His eyes study mine. "So is it okay if I call you Dini?"

He wants to have a special nickname for me? Why??? "Um, yeah. Sure. Do you not like Adina?"

"Of course I like Adina. It's a beautiful name. But Dini feels more…you. You can call me Josh."

My heart rate picks up. He wants me to call him Josh. It seems like only the people he's close to call him that. Why would he tell me to do so, too?

I bend my fingers in my lap. "Is that what your friends and family call you?"

"Yeah mostly. Not my parents, though. That's why I like when people call me Josh. Yehoshua reminds me of all the times I made trouble and got the 'Yehoshua Markus, you come in here this minute!' yell."

I find myself giggling. Then I feel self-conscious because he told me he thinks my laugh is cute.

"I wasn't exactly a well-behaved kid in school," he says. "My brothers told me everything they could about my teachers, since they had them before me. I knew exactly what to do to push their buttons." He shakes his head as he chuckles. "I was impossible."

"The poor teachers," I say with a smile.

He laughs again. "Yeah."

Quiet.

Why does this always happen? We go from having fun, interesting conversations to total silence. It's frustrating. And what exactly does he want from me? I don't understand this guy.

"So you cook," he says.

"I can follow a recipe," I offer, then find myself laughing. "Sorry. All this laughing is making me a little hyper."

"That's good. Laughter is healthy. You seem, um. Well, you seem sad a lot."

"I do?"

He looks uncomfortable. "Not that I'm studying you or anything. But you seem to be down sometimes."

I look at my lap. "Oh. Well...It just sucks when, like, when um..."

"I'm sorry if I pried."

"No, it's okay. It's just...well, dating sucks."

Understanding enters his eyes. "Indeed it does."

I'm bursting to ask him so many questions. Is he having a difficult time getting dates? Has he dated anyone seriously? What kind of girls does he like? But it's none of my business.

We're once again bathed in silence. Yehoshua gathers Greene's documents that are lying on his desk and makes them into a neat pile. I glance at my watch. "Wow."

"What?"

"It's 5:30." Work ends at 5:00.

His eyes widen. "I'm sorry for keeping you."

"It's fine. Really." I want to add that it's fun talking to him, but I don't want to be too forward.

He hands me the papers. "Have a great evening."

"You, too."

I go back to my desk and realize the office is empty. Everyone has already gone home. I place Greene's papers in one of the drawers, then start packing up. As I'm putting on my jacket, Yehoshua steps out of his office. "Hey, Dini?"

The nickname. I really like it.

I turn around. "Yeah?"

"You take the bus home, right? Do you want a ride?"

"Oh, that's okay."

"Are you sure? I feel bad that I kept you an extra half hour. It's going to start getting dark soon and I know what a hassle traveling on the bus is."

He's not wrong about that—city buses can be pretty bad sometimes. But I've never ridden in a guy's car before, other than when I was on a date. But this isn't a date. No, it's just a harmless ride from my coworker. He's just being nice. It means *nothing*.

"Dini?" he asks.

"Okay, thanks."

"Just give me a second to lock up. Meet me outside?"

"Okay."

As I wait, I can't help but feel nervous. I'm going to be in a car with Yehoshua. But it means nothing. *Nothing*.

The door opens, and he walks out. He gives me a smile before locking up. "I'm parked around the corner."

That Special Someone

We don't say anything as we make our way to the car. I don't mind the silence. I know some people can't stand it and have a need to say something, but the quiet feels peaceful.

Yehoshua stops before a silver car. He unlocks it and opens the passenger door for me. "Thanks," I tell him, feeling like this *is* an actual date. Yehoshua climbs in and buckles up.

The car smells really good. I've been in many guys' cars, and some of them didn't smell pleasant. That wasn't a reason for me to reject a guy, though, but a good smell does make the ride more enjoyable.

"Where to?" he asks.

I tell him my address.

He starts the car. We're both quiet as he drives. I don't realize I'm wringing my hands in my lap until my nail scratches my skin. I fist them and lay them on my knees. I don't want Yehoshua to think I'm uncomfortable. I'm just really nervous.

"Okay," he says after a few more minutes of silent driving. "Tell me a random fact about yourself." His eyes are on the road, but they flit to me for a second before focusing back on the road.

"Um…" I feel my heart pound nervously. I don't do well when I'm put on the spot. "I can't think of anything."

"I'll start, then. My random fact is that I slept with a nightlight until I was sixteen."

"Really?"

He laughs, embarrassed. "Yeah. We had a burglar in our house when I was really little. Thank God no one was home and they didn't steal anything too valuable, but I couldn't sleep for weeks. I would always have nightmares. I'm glad I got over the fear, because I doubt my wife would appreciate sleeping with a nightlight every night."

"I wouldn't mind," I find myself saying. Then I feel my eyes grow bigger than the wheels of this car. Oh my gosh, what did I just *say*?

His cheeks grow deep red. They most definitely match the color of mine.

"I m-mean," I stammer. "When I was a kid, I used to run around the house with only underwear on."

Now my eyes are bigger than the whole car. What did I just *admit*? I was so focused on changing the subject that I blurted out one of the most embarrassing stories of my life.

But Yehoshua doesn't look repulsed or shocked. He laughs softly. "That's actually pretty cute. My niece is like that, too. Except, she'd rather run around the house without any clothes on."

I feel my cheeks get back their natural color and my heart rate slows down. "How old is she?"

"Two. She's adorable. Ah, I love her. I love all my nieces and nephews, but not as much as my Shevy Monster. Don't tell them I said that, though."

He's good with kids. That's an A plus. Not that it matters. Nope.

"She sounds really cute," I say.

He nods. "She is."

Silence.

"Are we still playing?" I ask.

"Hmm?" He glances at me for a second before looking back at the road.

"The random embarrassing fact question game."

"Oh! Okay, my turn. Hmm. I need to think." He lightly taps his fingers on the steering wheel. "You promise you won't tell this to anyone?"

"I promise."

"Okay. I used to steal my sisters' dolls and pretend they were heading to the guillotine. So I would take the sharpest knife we had in the house and…well you can imagine the rest."

"Oh my gosh! Your poor sisters. My oldest brother did that to my dolls, too! Except, he would tear off their heads. I would cry for hours."

He laughs, then frowns. "Now I feel bad."

"You should," I say, my tone light and playful. "What did your sisters do to deserve it?"

"They probably messed up my Lego or something."

I shake my head in a serious fashion, but I can't help the smile on my lips.

"Your turn," he says.

"Okay, I got one. I used to take scissors and cut my mother's *sheitels*."

His jaw falls open. "No."

I nod eagerly. "Yes! My mom wanted to kill me."

"I don't blame her."

We both start laughing.

"I can imagine it," he says, still laughing. "Not that I know what she looks like. But I can imagine her spending so much money on a beautiful wig, and then one day she comes home from work and it looks like a haircut gone wrong."

We both continue to laugh. My stomach hurts and my eyes tear. When I calm down, I realize Yehoshua has stopped the car. We're in front of my house. "Oh, we're here," I say.

He's looking at me with an unreadable expression on his face.

"Thanks for the ride."

He blinks. "No problem. I…I had fun. You're fun."

My heart rate starts to race again. "Thanks. You're fun, too."

"Thanks." He taps his fingers on the steering wheel again. "Well, good night, Dini."

"Good night, Yehoshua." I put my hand on the door handle.

"Josh, please," he says.

My hand freezes. "Josh."

He smiles. He really has such a nice smile.

"Dini?"

I snap out of it. Was I staring at him?

"You okay?" he asks.

"Yeah. I'll leave now. Bye," I mutter, opening the door.

"Bye."

Before closing the door, I say, "Enjoy the *sheva brochos*. And the yummy Chinese food."

He nods. "Will do."

I close the door and march up to my house. Mom's not home because she's working the night shift. I find leftovers from last night's dinner in the fridge and warm it up. As I'm eating, all I think about is Yehoshua—I mean, Josh. I don't understand him. He seems like such a nice person, very considerate and engaging. But what exactly are his intentions? He said he doesn't want to go out with any of his coworkers. I don't want to be strung along and have my heart broken. And I can't forget Miriam's words, that he's difficult. She said he doesn't take people's feelings into consideration, but he certainly has taken mine. I know I'm not supposed to understand guys because they're from another planet, but I'm totally lost here. I'm not ashamed to admit that I like him. A lot. But can you blame me? He seems to like me, the clumsy awkward girl who always finds the opportunity to embarrass herself. No guy I've dated has come close to Josh.

Have I finally found my special someone, or is he going to throw me to the curb like everyone else?

Chapter Fourteen

I'm in a very good mood the next morning. My hair finally cooperates when I let it hang loose down my shoulders in neat waves. I dress into one of my favorite outfits—a purple top with a matching purple skirt that has cool designs. I don't put on any makeup, besides for blush. I like the way I look naturally.

Okay, I'll admit it. I'm looking forward to seeing Josh at work. I couldn't stop thinking about him when I went to bed last night. I just...I've never felt such a connection to a guy before. I've went out with so many, and while most of them were kind and pleasant, I didn't feel like I had a deep connection to them. It's different with Josh. He makes me not afraid to be myself.

A little voice in my head reminds me that Josh made it

perfectly clear that he has no intention of going out with any of his coworkers. But I don't listen to it. I'm just in such a good mood and I don't want anything to bring me down.

Even the bus ride goes smoothly. There is hardly anyone on it, so I get to work earlier by fifteen minutes. The door is locked, which means I'm the first one. I dig my key out of my bag and open the door. After turning on the lights and hanging my jacket, I settle down at my desk and continue working on Greene's tax returns, humming.

"Someone seems to be in a good mood," Miriam's voice says. I look up and find her standing before me with a large grin. "You were humming."

"Sorry. I probably made your ears bleed."

"Not at all." She drops down on her desk. "You have a good voice."

"I must be off or something."

She laughs. "So can I ask what has you in a good mood?"

My face flushes. "Well, um. You can probably guess."

Her eyes fill with light. "You had a good date last night?"

Close. "Sort of."

She claps her hands. "I'm so happy! I can't wait to see you engaged. You deserve an amazing guy."

That Special Someone

I hold out my hands. "One step at a time, please."

The little voice in my head nags me again. I don't want to listen to it. I just want to live in bliss for a little bit longer.

The other girls start filing in, followed by Mr. Markus and Josh. Our eyes lock, and he smiles. I return one, maybe a bit too enthusiastically. When I glance down at the document I'm working on, I find the page a little damp from my palm. I wipe it on my skirt.

The hours go by. When I have a few questions to ask Josh, I head to his office. He's sitting back and balancing an eraser on his nose. As soon as I knock and walk in, he drops the eraser and starts typing on his keyboard. When he realizes it's me, he says, "I wasn't bored. I was wondering if I could balance an eraser on my nose. Turns out I can."

I laugh. "I have a few questions."

"Fire away."

I do, and when I'm done he says, "Anything else?"

"Yeah. How was *sheva brochos*?"

"A little crazy with all the kids running around. But the food was great."

I frown. "You're making me so hungry."

He frowns, too. "Sorry."

Quiet.

I gather the papers. "I'll come back if I have any more questions."

He inclines his head. I walk to the door and close my hand over it. But it doesn't open all the way and I end up smacking my face into it. "I'm okay," I tell him, laughing, totally embarrassed. "My nose is okay."

He laughs, too.

I mutter under my breath as I'm heading back to my desk, reprimanding myself for once again being a klutz in front of him. I know my clumsiness can get annoying—it annoys *me*. I don't want Josh to be annoyed, too.

I don't want to seem like I'm obsessed with him or anything, so I don't go to see him for the rest of the morning. I work on my game during lunch while I chow down another peanut butter and jelly sandwich. When I get back to work, I hear yelling coming from Mr. Markus's office.

It's Mr. Markus and Josh. I can't make out what they're saying, but they are definitely yelling.

When I look at Miriam, I see her exchanging glances with the others. They don't look as surprised as me, as though this happens every day. I can't help but cringe when I hear Josh raise his voice.

Mr. Markus's door swings open. Josh marches into his office and slams the door behind him. Mr. Markus doesn't come after his son. His door slowly swings shut.

The office is dead silent.

Someone shuffles a piece of paper.

Someone uses a stapler.

Someone sneezes.

Josh's door flies open. He walks to the copy machine with a scowl, makes a copy, and walks away, not looking at anyone or anything.

We continue working in silence.

I'm so curious to know what happened between them, but of course it's none of my business. All family members fight—there's nothing weird about that. But it did sound like a pretty intense argument.

An hour later, I have some questions to ask Josh. I really don't want to bother him. I try to continue working despite that, but after a few minutes I realize I can't move on unless my questions are answered. I pull myself off my chair and go to Josh's office. His door is shut. I knock before stepping in. He's leaning forward, his elbows resting on his desk and his head buried in his hands. I freeze in place. It's obvious this is *not* a good time.

As I turn around to leave, the floor creaks beneath my feet. Josh's head snaps up, his eyes flashing to me. It looks like he has tears in them.

He straightens. "Yeah?"

"S-sorry, I'll leave."

"You have a question?" His tone doesn't hold the friendliness he's always given me in the past. It's cold.

"Yeah." I move closer to lay the papers out in front of him, but his cold behavior causes my hands to shake. The papers slip, falling on the desk and floor.

I drop down to gather them.

"You know something?" he says from above me. "Just leave everything. I'll finish the returns."

I pop up from the floor. "What? But—"

"I'll do it. You can leave." He turns to his computer.

I just gape at him, not believing what I'm hearing. He's being so rude. I understand that he's upset because of what happened with his dad, but I never expected he'd talk to me in this manner.

He turns toward me. "Please."

That Special Someone

I nod before walking to the door. My hand touches the doorknob, but I don't turn it. I look back at him. "Josh, are you okay?"

He clicks the mouse.

"Josh."

"Can you please leave my office?" His tone is not gentle. Nor are his eyes.

I swallow and hurry out. I don't care how upset he is—he has no right to speak to me like that. I just wanted to know if he was okay, if he wanted to talk. I wanted him to know I was here for him. I know we aren't like…together or anything, but I feel like I've been slapped across the face.

Pathetic, really. I shouldn't feel so hurt by his rejection. But the fact that I do makes me feel even more pathetic. I do care. A lot. And I'm hurt. Deeply.

Maybe Yehoshua Markus isn't the guy I thought he was.

Chapter Fifteen

I text Avigayil and ask her if she wants to hang out after work. She meets me at the ice cream shop a few blocks away from my office. She orders butter pecan ice cream while I get a blueberry milkshake. We settle down at one of the tables in the back of the shop.

I haven't stopped thinking about Josh. I hate that I keep replaying what happened in his office over and over again in my head. I find myself defending his behavior, convincing myself he didn't mean to act the way he did, that he was just upset. I *did* see him crying after all. But he didn't apologize. I waited and hoped he'd come out of his office and say he's sorry, but he stayed inside for the rest of the day, only leaving to use the bathroom.

And I can't forget the fact that he took over Greene's tax

returns. Mr. Markus specifically told him that we should work on them together. And I also can't forget the flash of annoyance I saw on his face when I accidentally dropped the papers. I've seen that expression one too many times on people, but I never thought I'd see it on him. I thought he was okay with my awkwardness.

Why did he have to be kind to me? Why did he make it seem like he was interested? Why on Earth do I care? He shouldn't mean anything to me. *Anything.* But in the few days following his sister's wedding, he made me feel different than any guy ever had. He made me feel happy to be me. He made me think it's possible someone could like me.

I shake my head. I need to forget about him.

"Okay, what's up?" Avigayil says, pulling me out of my thoughts.

"Huh?"

She digs her spoon in her cup of ice cream and dumps it in her mouth. Her face shines with pure delight. "My gosh, how I miss this! I'm so going to pay for these extra calories, but they are *so* worth it."

That makes me smile. Only for a little bit. I take a sip of my milkshake.

"Seriously, Adina. What's going on? You look so sad."

I shake my head and take another sip. "It's nothing."

"I smell guy problems."

I don't say anything, just drink some more.

"Is it the boss's son?"

I nod.

She puts her hand over mine. "What happened?"

"Me, that's what happened. I thought…I mean…" I sigh. "I guess I was living in a fantasy world."

"What do you mean?"

I tell her everything that happened, starting with how he talked to me at the wedding and ending with how he acted toward me today. "Am I blowing things out of proportion?" I ask. "I mean, he *was* upset with his father. I think he might have been crying."

"Maybe," she says. "But that still didn't give him the right to speak to you the way he did."

I take a long sip of my milkshake. "It's my fault. I shouldn't have started having feelings for him. All it took is for him to show an ounce of kindness and I was pulled in."

She rubs my hand. "It's because you want to meet someone who will love you so badly. And you deserve to meet someone like that. But you have to be careful not to fall for the wrong person."

"So." I swallow. "You're saying Josh—I mean, Yehoshua Markus—isn't the right person?"

"No. I'm saying you need to be careful before you give your heart to someone. Make sure he's the right one. Make sure he treats you right. Make sure he accepts you for who you are, not who he wants you to be." She rubs my hand again. "Only you can decide if someone is the right guy for you. Just make sure he deserves you."

I nod as I take her words in. I've dated many guys and have usually been able to tell right away if a guy was the right one for me. But I have no idea what to make of Josh. If he were any other guy, I would forget about him in a heartbeat. But he isn't any other guy. He's different. That's what makes this so confusing.

But I don't need this. It's not like we were even going out—he specifically stated that he didn't want to date any of his coworkers. If we continued the way we did, I would have ended up being hurt either way. Maybe it's for the best that this happened now instead of a few weeks down the road. It would hurt more.

"The best thing for you to do," Avigayil says, "is to get back out there and meet a sweet guy."

"As if that's so easy," I mutter.

"You know what they say. With each guy that doesn't work out, you get closer and closer to the right one."

"My soulmate must have lost his map because he's taking a really, *really* long time to get to me."

She laughs softly. "See, that's what I love about you. Even when you're feeling down, you manage to have a sense of humor."

"Thanks."

We continue eating and sipping. I want to forget about Josh—I mean, Yehoshua. I don't know how I'll get through the days, but hopefully from this point forward he and I will have as little interaction as possible. Considering he's taken complete control over Greene's returns, I have no reason to speak to him anymore.

Of course if he tries to talk to me…

No. The best thing is to forget him. Even if he does apologize, I need to. Because he has no intention of going out with me, and I don't want to get mixed up in a platonic relationship which never remain platonic. The guy or the girl will eventually get hurt. In this case, the bets are on me.

"So have you gone out with Shmuli Lerer?" I ask Avigayil.

She nearly chokes on her ice cream as her entire face lights up, as though there are ten lightbulbs buried in her skull. "I did!"

"Well what are you waiting for? Spill!"

Her face turns bright red. She seems to lose her appetite because she pushes her ice cream cup aside. She looks like she has hearts in her eyes. "He came over with flowers," she says, her voice dreamy. "He later admitted that his older brother advised him not to bring me flowers because while we're serious, we haven't been dating that long, but he didn't listen to him. I guess he's a romantic. I was so shocked and excited! Then he took me into the city and we took a horse-drawn carriage ride around Central Park."

I feel jealousy brewing in the pit of my stomach, but I shove those selfish feelings aside. I'm happy for Avigayil. Really, truly happy. She deserves the best. Even though I've always dreamed of marrying a romantic guy, I don't want to have any ill thoughts toward Avigayil. With God's help, I'll meet the right one day. Even if he may not be romantic. All that matters is that he's kind and that he accepts me for me.

"I have to admit it was awkward in the beginning," Avigayil says. "We've never been in such a closed, private space before, other than when we were in his car, but this was totally different. It made me feel special." Her face flushes again.

"I'm so happy for you! I wouldn't blame you for falling in love with him just because of that."

If her face were any redder, she'd be a tomato. "Wait, wait, wait. Who said anything about falling in love?"

I laugh. "If he keeps this up, I bet you'll fall in love with him in only a few days."

She laughs, too, her cheeks still red.

A hard swallow makes its way down my throat. I chug down some more of my milkshake.

"You'll meet him soon," she tells me. "I promise."

"It's not a promise you can make."

"But I know you'll meet him soon. I just know it."

"Thanks."

***

Programming reminds me of him. I push my laptop aside and fall down on my bed, locking my fingers behind my head and staring at the ceiling. The ceiling that is peeling and is in a desperate need of a paint job.

That Special Someone

Yehoshua sort of became my inspiration, my drive to work on my game. But now all I get is bile in my throat when I turn on the program. I hope I get over this soon because I don't want anyone or anything to get in the way of my dreams. Even though the thought of working on my game nearly sends me to the bathroom, I still love it. I can't wait until Yehoshua is buried deep in the recesses of my mind. Maybe I'll meet another guy by then, someone who will love my work and will motivate me to keep going. That would be awesome. It's what I need now. Like Avigayil said, I need to get back out there and meet a good guy.

I glance at the clock on the wall and see it's only 7:00 PM. I'm bored out of my mind. I reach for the novel I'm reading and open to the spot I'm up to. But after only a few minutes, I snap it shut and put it aside. Reading reminds me of him, too.

Ugh. Ugh. Ugh.

After pulling myself off my bed, I make my way downstairs and reach for one of the cookbooks sitting on the counter. I think I'm in the mood of a chocolate cake. Yeah, this occasion definitely calls for that. I'm not the greatest baker, so I leaf through the pages in search for a simple recipe. When I find it, I throw on an apron and gather the ingredients.

Half an hour later, the cake is baking and I'm covered in flour. So are the counter and floor.

I hear the sound of keys, followed by the door opening. Mom walks in. Her whole face fills with surprise when she sees me. "Did you attack my kitchen?" she jokes.

I take off my glasses and wipe them with the hem of my shirt. "Be nice or I won't let you have from my chocolate cake."

"Chocolate cake! What's the occasion?"

"Um…" I busy myself with cleaning the countertop. "No reason. Just bored. How was work?"

She sighs as she falls onto a chair. She looks exhausted. I feel bad because I know I contribute to some of the stress in her life. "Busy," she says. "And my boss yelled at me." She rubs her temples. "I just want to relax with a good book and some chocolate cake."

"Okay. But I can't promise it'll be edible."

"I'm sure it's delicious."

I concentrate on wiping the counter. Mom relaxes at the table.

"Um, Mom?"

"Yes, sweetie?"

That Special Someone

"I think I'm ready to date again."

She straightens up in her chair, her whole face washing with joy. "You are?"

I nod. Hopefully I'll meet someone so special I'll forget all about Yehoshua Markus.

Mom scrambles to her feet, all excited. "I'll call Mrs. Shain right away."

I nod again, my throat tight. I don't know if I'll ever meet anyone who makes me feel the way he did, but I need to try. I need to have faith.

When the cake is done, I pull it out of the oven. It looks delicious. I cut a slice for myself and Mom, who is still talking to the matchmaker. When I bite into it, I close my eyes and sigh. It tastes just as good as it looks.

Chapter Sixteen

Standing in front of the office, I tell myself to relax. Yehoshua is just a coworker, that's it. If he and I wouldn't have had such a connection, we would have just been pleasant to one another without having to exchange too many words.

I take a deep breath, let it out, and open the door. Naomi's sitting at her desk. When I crane my neck toward Yehoshua's office, I see the lights are closed. He's not here yet.

Naomi's eyes catch mine for a second, narrowing. She looks away, to her computer screen. I should tell her that she and I are in the same boat, that we like the same guy who rejected us. But of course I don't. I sit down at my desk and continue working on the bank statements I started yesterday, after Yehoshua decided to take over Greene's tax returns. I hope Mr. Markus won't assign us a project again.

That Special Someone

The others pile in, and my heart starts to pound. I don't want him to walk through the doors. I don't want to face him.

As I'm typing on my computer, the door swings open and Mr. Markus walks in. He stops before my desk. "Good morning, Adina. How's it going with Greene's returns?"

"Um…"

"Don't tell me my son is slacking off."

"Um, no. We're working on them." At least, one of us is. Mr. Markus doesn't seem to be upset with his son anymore.

"Good, good. Good morning, girls!"

They return the greeting. He disappears into his office.

My feet twitch.

An hour passes. Another half hour passes. Maybe he won't come in today.

Because of me? I scoff to myself. Sure, as if I'm the center of his life. He might still be upset with his father.

At lunchtime, as I'm browsing online and eating my sandwich, Yehoshua walks inside. He closes the door softly behind him and stands there with his back facing the rest of us. After a few seconds, he turns around and our eyes meet.

We both quickly look away.

I peek at him and find him doing the same. Seeing his

face…it's hard to not feel the way I did the past few days when we were getting friendly. I force my eyes away again. He does the same.

As he passes my desk, I raise my eyes to his and see them trekking to mine. A part of me hopes he'll stop and give me a smile. That he'll apologize and ask me to meet in his office. That he still wants my help with Greene's tax returns. But he does no such thing. He just continues on to his office.

I feel my body sag with disappointment. He didn't apologize.

That proves he's not the right guy for me. Maybe what Miriam and all the other girls claimed is really true, that he's not considerate of other people's feelings and is unsympathetic. I didn't want to believe them because he was so kind and considerate to me.

I shake my head. It doesn't matter.

I don't see him for the rest of the day. He hardly leaves his office.

Instead of taking the bus home, I decide to visit Henny. I haven't spoken to her much since we went shopping last week. She answers the door, all frazzled, her wig askew, her clothes rumpled. Penina is crying in her arms and Akiva is hanging onto her ankles, screaming at the top of his lungs. I hear Tehila yelling from inside.

Henny looks at me as though I'm her salvation. She dumps Penina in my arms and unlatches Akiva from around her ankles. He continues to wail, which causes Tehila to wail as well.

"What's going on?" I ask as I follow her into the house. She places Akiva on the couch. He kicks his legs in the air, still yelling. Tehila leaps onto the couch and copies her brother.

"Look at what they did to the wall," Henny says, her face haggard. I peer to my left and see the wall covered in paint. "I promised them candy if they behaved themselves, but after seeing this?"

"I want candy!" Akiva cries. "Candy!"

I sit down on the recliner with Penina on my lap. She's still crying. I hug her close.

"We'll just wait it out," Henny tells me. "They'll give up soon. And hopefully pass out from exhaustion."

When I see days like this, I wonder if I want to be a mom. But I know I do. As tiring and frustrating as it can be, I know having kids is one of the most rewarding things in life.

I'm pretty sure Tehila isn't really upset—she's just copying her older brother. I call her name and tell her to climb onto my lap. She continues kicking her legs in the air. "Come on, Tehila," I say, tapping my knee. She kicks her legs a few more times before rolling off the couch and hopping onto my lap. I hold both her and her sister close in my arms. I kiss the top of their heads.

"Akiva said it would be fun to paint the house," Tehila says. "Just like the painting men did." She's referring to a few weeks ago, when Henny and Dov hired people to paint a few walls in their house.

"Painting is fun," I tell her. "Just next time, ask Mommy before you do anything, okay?"

"Akiva said we could."

"Akiva should have asked Mommy."

She pouts.

Henny massages her lower back.

"How's your back?" I ask.

"Not that great. I have an appointment at the doctor tomorrow. Akiva, stop yelling!"

"No! I want candy!"

"I'll play a game with them," I tell her, lowering Tehila to the floor and getting up. I place Penina in the playpen and tell

Tehila to go to her room. Then I sweep Akiva off the couch and follow his sister. He kicks at me, causing me to almost drop him, but I tighten my hold and lower him to the floor of their room.

"Candy!"

"We're going to play a game now."

"No! I want candy!"

I search through the board games and settle on one. Then I set it up on the floor. Tehila drops to her knees and starts playing with the pieces.

"Akiva, don't you want to play?" I ask.

"No!"

"Okay. Suit yourself."

He sobs in the corner of the room as Tehila and I play the game. I feel so bad for him, but it's not my place to step in and parent him.

Luckily, it doesn't take too long for Akiva to calm down and join us. After a few minutes, they are both well-behaved and playing nicely. I tell them to play by themselves and go to the living room to look for Henny. She's resting on the couch.

I sit down on the recliner. "You okay?"

"Thanks for quieting them down."

"No problem. They're playing a game."

She closes her eyes and breathes in and out softly.

"How are things with Dov?" I ask. "Or would you rather not talk about it?"

Her eyes are still shut, but I see the anxiety on her face. "I tried talking to him last night. I think I just drove him further away."

"I'm sorry."

She puffs out some air. "It's like he doesn't want to try and make our marriage work. Whenever I start talking about something serious, he tunes me out or walks away. He's never been like that before."

I don't know what to say. I have no clue what goes on in a man's head. I can't even get a guy to go out with me a third time. And I won't even *think* about Yehoshua's mind.

"He's stressed," Henny continues. "We both are. Life is stressful."

"But you have someone to share it with. Don't forget that. There are so many people out there wishing they had someone they can share their life with."

Henny's eyes slowly open and move to mine. Her face fills with guilt and sympathy. "You're right. I'm so sorry for complaining about my marriage when you—"

I hold out my hand. "Just because you're married when there are many people out there still single, you have the right to vent if you need to. I guess I was just trying to help by making you see the positive."

She carefully sits up and reaches for my hand. "No, you're right. Sometimes I get so caught up in the little things in life that I don't see the big picture. Thank God I have a caring husband who is a phenomenal father. My kids are, thank God, healthy. I don't even know what I'm complaining about. Thanks for helping me see the positive, Adina."

"You're welcome."

Chapter Seventeen

After I get back from Henny's, I sit at my computer and work on my game. It still reminds me of Yehoshua, but my love for programing triumphs over that. I want to get over him. I still think about him a lot, but I know I'll eventually stop. I'm confident that I will soon meet the right guy for me, God willing.

I'm so absorbed in my work that I don't hear Mom walk into my room until she stands before me. I nearly jump to the ceiling from fright. "Mom! You scared me." I clutch my chest as my heart races so fast I think it may bullet out of me.

"I'm sorry. I was calling you for supper."

"Oh." I look at my computer screen. I'm in the middle of something and can't leave right now.

"I'll bring it up to you," she says.

That Special Someone

"It's okay. I'll come soon."

"Okay."

As I continue working, trying to finish as fast as possible, Mom returns to my room, balancing a bowl of soup and a plate filled with chicken and a baked potato in her hands.

"Mom, you didn't have to do that." I take the food from her and place it on the night table.

She strokes my hair. "I know how engrossed you are when you're working on your game. Just make sure to get a few bites in."

I get up to her hug. "Thanks, Mom. You're the best. I love you."

"Love you, too." She gives me a smile before kissing my forehead and leaving.

I don't think I would be able to get through this dating process without her. Actually, I wouldn't be able to get through my life without her. After my father left, I knew she was hurting. He didn't only abandon his kids, he abandoned his wife as well. He left her with five kids and she had to take on both the mother and father roles, and support us all by herself. I just wish I could repay her. I don't know how. I always thought finding a good guy to settle down with would do the trick, but that hasn't happened yet. Hopefully soon.

Not wanting the soup to get cold, I gobble it down before continuing to work. When I'm done, I finish my meal, then open a webpage. I type in "Ephraim Reid" in the search bar. Like all the other times I've searched my father's name, I don't receive any results. My father really has disappeared from the face of the planet. I have no idea if he's even alive. I kind of feel deep down that he is. I bet he's married and has another family somewhere. I bet he doesn't think about me and my siblings.

No. I know he does think about us, wherever he is. The good thing about not knowing where he is or what he's doing is that I can fabricate my own story. Ever since I was little, I told myself that Dad has a secret government job, like he's part of the CIA or something. I doubt that's a real possibility, though, because it would be extremely difficult to be a CIA agent and an observant Jew, but it beats the other scenario in my head. That my dad left us because he stopped loving us. That he wanted to try again with a new wife and kids.

A part of me hopes I'll never look into his face again. That part swears to never forgive him for what he put us through. But the other side of me yearns to meet him one day. To look into his face and demand an explanation. *How could you leave your wife and kids? Did you stop loving us? Did you stop loving me?*

I stopped praying to God to send my dad back when I was fifteen. I figured if he didn't want to return to us, there was no point in asking Hashem to help. After all, a person needs to have the will if he wants God's help. I can't ask Hashem to force my dad to come back. If I'm not good enough for my father, then he doesn't deserve to be part of my life anymore.

***

Yehoshua is already in his office when I arrive the next day. I settle down at my desk and get to work. This may sound strange, but work seems to be a bit...boring. Not that I don't appreciate and enjoy my job anymore, but I used to look forward to talking to Yehoshua. Now I feel like a part of me has been lost.

The other girls and Mr. Markus arrive, and the day carries on as usual. At lunchtime, I rummage in my bag for my much-anticipated peanut butter and jelly sandwich, but I can't seem to find it. I wrack my brain, trying to remember if I made my sandwich. The memories slowly come to me. I cried a bit last night when I thought about my father. It felt good to let everything out, but I felt so tired afterward. I must have fallen asleep. Which means there is no sandwich for Adina.

I'm starving.

I put my papers in a neat pile, sling my bag over my shoulder, and stand up. "I'm going to buy some lunch," I tell Miriam. "Any suggestions?"

"Ooh, try Mendel's Delight. It's across the street from the park."

"The park?"

She looks at me like I asked her if cows fly. "You don't know there's a park around the corner?"

I laugh sheepishly and scratch my shoulder. "I haven't really explored the area. I just know the path from here to the bus..."

She laughs. Really hard. "Adina, you are something else."

She tells me the exact location of the deli. I don my jacket and leave the office. The weather's pretty nice today. I walk around the corner and see a park in the distance. It takes up most of the entire block. There are swings and a playground. Across from it, I see a large sign with the words "Mendel's Delight."

Only a few feet away, I smell onions and chicken. My stomach rumbles and my mouth waters. I quicken my pace and enter the restaurant. It's full. I grab a menu and wait on line. There are so many options. After looking it over for a few minutes, I settle on a burger and fries. Once I get my order, I search the area for a place to sit, but I'm not too surprised to discover there are no available tables. It is lunchtime after all. I ask the guy behind the counter to pack my food "to go" and decide to sit in the park to eat.

There is a small area with tables and chairs. I wash my hands before settling down and unwrapping my sandwich. It looks delicious. I take a large bite and my mouth explodes with all these amazing flavors. But my mouth isn't the only thing that's exploded. My sandwich has as well. It's stuffed with so many goodies that they slide out of the bread and fall onto the table. My fingers are dirty.

Well, messy things are usually the things that taste best. I take another large bite of the burger, trying to ignore the second mess I'm creating, when a tall man with dark hair walks into the park. I almost choke. Yehoshua Markus.

What's he doing here?

He scans around the park before his eyes find me. *Turn around*, I beg. *Turn around and leave.* But he doesn't. He heads straight for me.

I drop my sandwich and rummage in the Mendel's Delight bag for a few napkins. I manage to wipe my hands and mouth before he stops right in front of me. I notice he has a Mendel's Delight bag, too.

"Hi," he says, giving me a hesitant smile.

My mouth is too dry for me to say anything. I merely nod.

"Can I…" He nods to one of the chairs surrounding my small table.

It takes a few seconds for my jumbled mind to comprehend what he's asking me. He wants to join me. He bought lunch, too. And he wants to join me. Why?

I nod and move my food aside to give him room.

"Thanks." He places his bag on the table and sits down across from me. My shoe taps on the ground as I watch him pull out a container filled with chicken and vegetables.

We're going to eat together? I've never dined with a guy before, since I haven't made it past a second date. I don't know what to do. I feel so awkward.

"Am I disturbing you?" he asks.

"N-no. But, um. What are you doing here?"

"On my way to the bathroom, I overheard you asking Miriam where to buy lunch." He rubs the back of his neck. "I really want to talk to you. In private."

"Okay…"

"I didn't want anyone to overhear."

"Okay," I say again, not knowing what else to say.

"But I didn't want to take you away from your lunch. I figured I'd buy some lunch, too, and talk to you. Is that okay? Because if you'd rather I leave, I will."

"No, don't leave. I mean, you don't have to leave."

He gives me a small, relieved smile. "Okay." He takes the lid off his container. "Would you like some?"

"No, thanks. I have my…well, I have my thing."

"Thing?"

"Just look at it. It kind of exploded."

His eyes light up as he laughs. "Looks delicious."

"It is."

He stabs a piece of chicken with his fork and takes a bite. "First off, I want to apologize for my behavior, Dini. I didn't mean to act that way to you. I'm so sorry." His eyes are beyond sincere.

I blink a few times. He apologized. That's what I wanted from him—an apology. I feel the wall I built around my heart start to crumble.

"I was upset," he continues. "My dad, he…" He shakes his head. "It doesn't really matter. I was just so upset."

"I wanted to see if you were okay," I say.

"I know. I really appreciate it. You're such a special person, Dini."

I shake my head. "No—"

"Yes. And I know I hurt you when I pushed you out of my office. It was eating at me these past two days."

"Why?" I whisper.

His eyes drop to his food. "You know why."

"Say it," I say, my voice a whisper again.

His eyes slowly move to meet mine. "You're different, Dini. I knew that from the first moment I saw you."

I play with my Mendel's Delight bag. "Different?"

"In a good way."

I don't know what to say.

"I didn't mean to hurt you. I hope you can forgive me."

"I do," I tell him. "I accept your apology."

His eyes fill with relief. "Thanks. It means a lot."

We're both quiet.

"I was so nervous to talk to you," he says. "I thought you hated me."

"I could never hate you."

He nods as he plays around with the chicken in his container. Then he looks at my burger. "Aren't you going to eat that?"

"Oh. Um." My cheeks warm up. "It won't exactly be a pretty sight."

"I don't mind."

But I do. I don't want to make a fool of myself in front of him.

"Really," he says with a grin. "You should see the way I eat burgers."

That makes me smile. "Okay. But don't watch me."

"I won't."

He keeps his eyes on his chicken as he eats. I pick up my burger and take another bite. It's so good that I take another bite, and another. When I look at Yehoshua—Josh—I find his eyes locked on mine.

I drop my burger. "You said you wouldn't look!"

He laughs. "I couldn't help myself."

"I'm so embarrassed."

"Don't be. I don't mind when a girl is a little messy. Actually, I prefer that to a girl who is always obsessed with looking good. Girls have a right to not be perfect all the time."

"You're just saying that."

He shakes his head. "No, I mean it. I once when out with a girl who constantly excused herself to go to the bathroom. Literally every fifteen to twenty minutes. I got nervous because I thought she wasn't feeling well. But it turned out she went to check her makeup."

"Are you serious?" I ask.

"One hundred percent."

"Wow. I don't even check my makeup once."

"I know," he says.

"What?" How could he possibly know that?

"I mean, I figure you wouldn't. You're not like other girls. You're your own person."

I take another bite of my burger because I don't know what to say. I don't even know how I feel. I'm so glad he and I are talking again. I missed him. A lot. Maybe that's weird because I haven't known him for long, but I really did miss talking to him. But I'm also confused and wary. What exactly are we?

"I mean that in the best way possible," he says. "It makes you unique and interesting."

"Apparently not," I mutter.

That Special Someone

"What?"

"I've never made it past a second date."

His fork freezes over some broccoli. His eyes shoot to mine. "Never?"

I shake my head.

"I find that hard to believe," he says. He stabs the broccoli before looking at me again. "You have problems getting dates?"

I squirm in my seat.

"Sorry," he quickly says. "That's none of my business." He bites into the broccoli, then lowers the rest of it back into the container. "I hate broccoli. I didn't know chicken with various vegetables included broccoli."

"I don't like it, either."

He smiles. "Is there anyone who does?"

"Well, my mom."

"Yeah. Mine, too."

We're both quiet again. I've finished my burger and am full, but I need to do something instead of just sitting here. I take out my fries. "Want some?"

"Sure, thanks."

I lay the carton in the middle of the table and hand him a

few ketchup packets. We each take a fry. Then I take another and he does, too. When I go for a third one, so does he. Our hands touch. I pull away like I've been shocked.

"Sorry," he says, his cheeks pink.

"It's okay."

Quiet.

I want to ask him so many questions. What does this mean? What are we? Does he just want to be friends? Does he want to go out with me? He did say he thinks I'm interesting and finds it hard to believe that I haven't been past a second date, but he isn't asking me out. He's not making any indication that he wants to date me. Is it because of his rule not to date his coworkers? Then what does he *want* from me? I don't get him. I wish I could slice his brain open and read what's inside.

But I don't want to say anything. What if I push him away? What if he's the kind of person who takes things slow? I don't want to drive him away. But I don't want to be dragged around, either.

"I didn't do Greene's returns," Josh says, pushing aside the broccoli in his container. "I want to continue working on them with you. If that's okay."

"It is."

That Special Someone

"Okay." He sweeps a fry out of the carton. "My dad thinks I'm slacking off."

"Do you, um…do you want to impress him?" I ask, then mentally scold myself. That is a personal question. Way too personal. "Never mind," I quickly say.

"Yeah," he says, his voice soft. "I do want to impress him. But not with accounting."

I wait for him to continue, but he just eats more chicken. Is he referring to his singing? But how could his dad not be impressed with it? I've only heard him sing once and thought he was phenomenal. Surely his dad agrees. Maybe Josh is referring to something else. I'm so curious, but I have no right to pry.

Glancing at my watch, I see it's past my lunch hour. "I have to get back," I tell him.

"Okay."

While I say grace after meals, Yehoshua cleans up, throwing out my wrappers as well. That's very kind of him. A warm feeling enters my heart. But I push it aside and focus on *bentching*. When I'm done, I say, "Thanks for throwing out my stuff."

"No problem. I packed your fries."

"Thanks." That warm feeling returns.

We leave the park, walking side by side. Like the time we headed for his car when he drove me home, we don't say anything to each other. The silence doesn't make me feel awkward this time, either.

Josh opens the door for me, giving me a sweet smile. I return it with a thank you. The girls eye us suspiciously, especially Naomi.

"So we'll continue discussing the tax returns in my office," Josh says. "Come see me when you're ready."

"Okay."

I'm about to go to my desk when Naomi says, "Adina, look how many papers need to be filed."

My eyes move to the bin. It's overflowing. "What? But I just filed yesterday."

"Sorry," Shaindy says, ducking her head. "I printed out a lot of things that need to be filed."

I try not to groan. I'm really looking forward to talking some more with Josh. I mean, I'm really looking forward to continue working on Greene with Josh.

Yeah, right.

The filing will take me all day, though.

That Special Someone

I heave the bin onto the table in the conference room and embark on my epic journey of filing. After what feels like hours but is probably only half an hour, I peer into the bin and see that I've hardly made a dent. I try not to groan again. I can push this off for tomorrow, but the pile will just grow bigger.

"Adina?" Yehoshua peeks his head inside. "Ah, there you are. Are you ready to go over—wow, you're filing all of *that*?"

I nod.

He steps into the room and heads over to the bin, looking inside. He whistles. "Do you need help?"

"Oh, that's okay."

He reaches into the bin and gathers a few papers in his hands, flashing me a grin. "I don't mind helping. We'll be done in no time."

"Thanks," I say.

He walks over to the file cabinet on the other side of the room.

We work in silence for a really long time. Actually, it's only fifteen minutes, but it definitely feels longer. Josh and I reach for the bin at the exact time. He steps back and says, "Go ahead."

"Thanks." I take another pile.

"Dini?"

I look up at him.

"Do you like bowling?"

"Bowling?"

His eyes fill with a bit of humor. "It's where you take a really heavy ball and try to knock down ten pins. It's said to be a lot of fun."

I give him a face. "I've bowled before."

He laughs.

"Why are you asking me that?"

"Well…" He fingers the edge of the bin. "Do you want to go? With me?"

Once again, I just stare at him, completely dumbfounded. Hundreds of thoughts run through my head. He wants to go bowling with me? Why?

"Like a date?" I ask. My face heats up. I shouldn't have asked that. Maybe he just meant as friends. But girls and guys in my community don't usually hang out.

Josh chuckles softly, his own face red. "Yeah, a date."

"But you don't date your coworkers."

He gives me a confused face.

"Well, Naomi spoke to you…Sorry, that's none of my

business."

He sighs before pulling out one of the chairs surrounding the table and sitting down. "After what happened with Suri…" He looks at me. "Do you know about her?"

I nod.

"I told myself not to get involved with any of my coworkers. I feel horrible for what happened. I wanted to leave, but my dad didn't let. Suri had no choice but to quit. It was too hard." He shakes his head, his eyes sad. "I don't want to put anyone else through that." He slowly lifts his eyes to mine. "But then I met you."

My heart is beating so hard my ears ring.

He gets up and moves closer to me, until he's standing only a few inches away. I can see how long his eyelashes are. I look away for a few seconds before returning my gaze to him. My heart is still pounding. "Like I told you before," he says. "You're different. I'd like to get to know you better. If that's okay with you."

I can hardly think straight due to the beating of my heart. My tongue is tied. "And if the same thing happens?" I ask. "If we don't work out?"

"I hope we do," he says. "I think we can. What do you

think?"

I lower my eyes to my shoes. "You're the only guy who seems to be okay with my, um, klutziness."

"I think it's adorable."

My eyes move to his. "Adorable?"

He smiles. "Yeah. I find it very attractive."

My cheeks boil.

"Sorry if that was too forward," he says.

I laugh awkwardly and rub my shoulder.

He clears his throat. "So is that a yes to the bowling? Do you want to get a matchmaker involved? I'd rather not, but it's up to you."

"I'd rather not, either."

"Okay, good. So it's a yes?"

"Yes, but I don't want to put your life at risk."

"My life at risk?"

I rub my shoulder again. "Well, there was an incident…A few years ago, I accidentally dropped a bowling ball on my friend's foot. Well, I guess she's an ex-friend now. She had to go to the ER." I can't meet his eyes.

"I'm willing to take the risk," he says. "For you, Dini."

My face lifts to his. I feel a smile tug my lips. "You really

216

don't care that I'm awkward and clumsy and say silly things most of the time?"

He returns the smile. "Not at all."

"Then I'd love to go on a date with you, Josh Markus."

Chapter Eighteen

It's Sunday afternoon. Josh will pick me up in only a few minutes.

Mom clasps the necklace around my neck and looks at me through my mirror. "Are you sure about this, Adina?"

"I'm sure."

"But we don't know anything about him or his family." Her eyebrows are wrinkled with worry.

I try to pat my hair to hold some of the frizz down, but it's useless. I didn't straighten my hair this time. Josh likes me the way I am—I don't have to change anything about myself.

"He's my boss's son and my coworker," I assure Mom. "I've gotten to know him. He's a good guy."

The wrinkles don't disappear. "I hope so. Do you want me to find out information about him just in case?"

That Special Someone

I reach to hug her. "I think I can trust my own judgment."

She cups my face in her hands. "I don't want you to get hurt."

I rest my hand over hers. "It's part of the process, Mom. I've never felt this way about the other guys I've been out with. Yehoshua is different. Maybe even the one."

A flicker of hope flashes across her face, but it's gone a second later. "I don't have a good feeling about this."

"You don't have to hold my hand anymore. I think for the first time, I feel really good about a guy."

She still looks unsure.

"I'll be okay, Mom."

Though still uncertain, she nods and kisses my forehead. "I can see how excited you are. It makes me a little excited, too."

The doorbell rings. I gasp as every single hair on my body stands on edge.

Here's here. Oh my gosh he's here.

In just a few minutes, he'll be in my house. And then he and I will be alone on a *date*.

Mom softly pats my cheek before going downstairs. I take a few deep breaths and smooth my hands down my outfit. It's a black shirt with gray designs, and a black skirt, though not my favorite one because we are going bowling and I don't want to risk it getting damaged. But it's still very pretty. I'm wearing some makeup and my finest jewelry.

I'm so *nervous*. Much more so than the other dates. I start pacing around my room, forcing my hands to my sides before they could run through my hair and mess it up. I keep picturing the next few moments in my head, how it will all play out. I've done this many times in the past and they never turned out the way I envisioned. The best thing to do is relax and let everything take its course.

Mom must be wondering where I am. I need to get myself downstairs. But I don't know if I can. Hanging out with Josh was nerve-wracking at times, but I didn't feel any pressure. Now I feel like the pressure is knocking me over like a tidal wave. We're not just going to hang out, we're going to see if we're right for each other for marriage. The added stress is sure to make me even clumsier.

He claimed he likes my klutziness. But will he eventually find it annoying? Every part of me hopes he'll come to love everything about me the more he gets to know me, but I don't have the best track record. His rejection would hurt the most.

But I can't think like that. I need to think positively. Maybe

That Special Someone

God has finally sent me my soulmate. I don't want to mess up my chances because of my insecurities.

"Adina?" Mom calls from downstairs.

Shoot. I've kept them waiting. I check myself in the mirror one final time, and once I think I look good, I take another deep breath and head downstairs. Josh should be sitting at the kitchen table, probably eating my chocolate cake. Mom told me she'd offer him some. I hope he likes it.

I can't get a good look at him from where I am. I'll basically be walking into the kitchen blindly. Taking another deep breath, I make my way inside. The first person I see is Mom, and I study her face closely, trying to determine if Josh has made a good impression. She seems impressed enough. When the floor creaks beneath my feet, his head whips toward my direction. He shoots to his feet, still clutching his fork which holds a piece of the cake. It splats to the table.

The fact that he's just as nervous as me calms me down a little. He gives me a warm and sweet smile. I return it. He's wearing a dark jacket and dark pants, his hair is combed, and his yarmulke sits neatly on his head. He looks really good.

"Hi," he says.

"Hi."

We walk to the door, where Josh opens it for me. I give him a nervous thank you, to which he responds with an equally nervous "You're welcome." It's actually really cute how nervous he is. I'm growing more at ease every second that passes.

His silver car is parked in the driveway. He opens the door for me, and I once again thank him.

The few seconds I'm alone in his car before he gets in give me the time I need to collect my thoughts. I tell myself to relax and enjoy the afternoon. I'm on a date with *Josh Markus*. I wanted this for so long. I don't want to think too far ahead, that this might be the guy I'll marry, but I feel so good about this. Even though my skin crawls with nerves, I feel an odd sense of relief. Because I'm on a date with Josh Markus.

He climbs in, shuts the door, and buckles up. I buckle up, too. He drops the key as he tries to stick it in the ignition. "Sorry. I'm a little clumsy today."

"Maybe my clumsiness is rubbing off on you," I say, half-joking, half-serious.

He laughs awkwardly. "Let's just say I'm really nervous."

"Me, too! But I always get nervous. Why, um, why are you? I mean, you…" I don't finish my sentence. I don't want to say what I'm thinking—that he's usually so confident and put together. "Never mind. I really should shut up when I'm this nervous."

He starts the car and glances at me. "No, it's okay. I don't want you to hold back on your thoughts. Please, tell me everything in your head. I really like hearing what you have to say. And, um…I'm really nervous because I want today to go well."

I lean my head back and say, "Me, too."

"There's no reason why it shouldn't," he quickly says. "I guess I'm just anxious." He coughs. "I think I'll just be quiet now."

I laugh lightly. "No, I actually like it. I mean, not that I like that you're nervous, but I like that I'm not the only one who feels uneasy."

He pulls out of the driveway and drives toward the bowling alley. "Honestly, I've never been this nervous since I went on my very first date."

"Oh. Sorry."

"No, it's a good thing."

"Well, this is the most nervous I've been, too."

His gaze moves to meet mine for a few seconds before

returning to the road. "I want to have fun, though. We both need to relax." He takes a deep breath and lets it out slowly. I do, too. Our eyes lock on one another and we laugh.

"So…bowling," he says.

"Yeah. I chose a skirt that's not too long so it doesn't reach the floor and one that's not too fancy so it doesn't get ruined." I rub my forehead. "Sorry. I don't want to bore you out talking about clothes."

"It's okay. I dressed into my suit and then realized how ridiculous I'd look wearing that in a bowling alley. So I changed."

I find myself giggling, and I can't stop. Which is silly because he didn't say anything that funny. I guess it's my nerves.

"What?" he asks.

Still giggling, I shake my head. "Sorry."

"No, really. What did I say?"

"Nothing. I think I'm losing it."

He starts laughing, too.

Then we're both dead silent.

That causes me to laugh again, which makes him laugh as well. My left side aches and my eyes tear.

That Special Someone

"Okay." I wipe my eyes. "I think I'm done."

"I don't mind hearing you laugh, Dini."

"Thanks. I don't mind hearing you laugh, either."

He smiles.

We're quiet. I run my hands up and down my lap.

"We're almost there," he says. "Hey, I never asked if you're good at bowling."

I wave my hand. "I'm lucky if I can knock down two pins. How about you?"

He's trying to hide a smile.

I almost slap his arm playfully, but thankfully, I don't. "I bet you're the best bowler in the world."

"Not the world," he jokes.

"Okay, but don't go easy on me. I want a fair game."

He nods. "As you wish."

The car slows down as the bowling alley comes into view. Josh parks in the lot. I've never been to this place before, but I don't bowl very often. A cold breeze whisks past me, and I shiver, clutching my jacket tighter around myself.

We walk into the bowling alley, and I realize the place is huge. I see other Orthodox Jews here, too. It's Sunday afternoon, and bowling is a great activity to do as a family or on a date. I just hope I don't meet any nosy friends or neighbors. Not that I'm embarrassed or ashamed to been seen with Josh, I just always feel uncomfortable when someone I know sees me on a date. They can't hide the curiosity and questions from their eyes—is this the man Adina Reid will marry? But that's just the way people are.

We decide to play two games. Once Josh pays and we receive our shoes, we make our way to the lane. Excitement pulses through me as I watch the other bowlers. It's really been a while since I've done this, and I'm really looking forward to it.

Josh and I sit side by side on the chairs and put on our shoes. "The best part of bowling," he jokes.

We walk to the machine to put in our names. Josh motions for me to take the seat. My hands freeze over the buttons. "Want to pick cool names?"

"Okay." He taps the area between his nose and mouth. "How about 'Awesome Programmer' for you."

That makes me laugh. "Okay." I type it in. "And I have the perfect name for you." I put in "Awesome Singer" and grin at him. He smiles, too, but it doesn't reach his eyes. I don't have a chance to linger on it because he looks up at the screen and says, "Here we go. You're up."

That Special Someone

I'm burning to ask him why he always gets that dark look whenever his singing is mentioned, but I'm worried I'll ruin the date. There's time to talk about heavy topics later, assuming there *is* a later. I hope so.

Josh picks up one of the balls. "Is this too heavy for you? I can look for a lighter one."

He hands it to me, and I nearly drop it. He quickly takes it from me, his skin brushing against mine. "Sorry," he says. "I'll look for a lighter ball."

"Thanks."

As he heads for the racks of balls, I feel my cheeks lift as I smile. He's very considerate. Definitely an A plus in my book.

He returns a few minutes later, holding an orange ball in one arm and a dark purple one in the other. I take the orange ball from him. "This one feels good," I say. I put it down and try the purple one. "This is good, too."

"Looks like we're all set." He glances up at the screen. "Ready?"

I nod. I don't know why I'm nervous for my first round. I mean, it's just a game. I guess I want to impress him. I walk to the lane and swing my arm, letting the ball free. It rolls straight for the middle, and I'm about to jump for joy, but it swerves left and falls right into the gutter.

Heading back to Josh, I frown. "Gutter ball."

His face lights up as he laughs. "You're so cute."

I feel myself blush. "Thanks. Maybe I'll have more luck with the purple one."

I hit one pin. When I turn around to Josh, he's clapping enthusiastically.

"Better than a gutter ball," I say.

He nods. "Definitely progress." He reaches for the black ball. "Here I go."

He throws the ball with so much energy that it shoots toward the pins, hitting them right in the center. They all get knocked down. Strike.

I don't know what has me more shocked—the fact that he got a strike, or that he's so strong.

He comes back with a proud but guilty expression. "Beginner's luck?"

I find myself blinking at him. "You're so strong."

He lowers his head, looking embarrassed. "I work out a lot. It helps me relieve stress."

Relieve stress? What kind is he talking about? I know everyone has stress in their lives and have things to deal with, but by the pained look in Josh's eyes, I have a feeling there's so much more. I can't ask him, though. He'll tell me when he's ready. I mean, assuming I manage to get past a second date. And a third possibly, maybe even a forth. However much time he needs.

"Dini?"

I shake my head, snapping myself out of my thoughts. "Yeah?"

"Your turn."

"Oh." I reach for the purple ball, my mind still trying to hang onto the thoughts that were swarming my mind. But they're long gone. I head to the lane and swing my arm, hoping to get a lot of momentum, just like Josh did. When I release the ball, it's definitely faster, but it just lands in the gutter faster, too.

I clutch my wrist as pain shoots through my hand. Ouch! I must have overdone it.

Josh's eyes are full of concern when I walk back to him. "Are you okay? Did you hurt yourself?" His eyes examine my hand. He raises his like he wants to touch me, but he drops it to his side.

"I'm fine," I assure him. It's not a lie because the pain is lessening. "I guess I'm more competitive than I thought."

His eyes remain on my wrist for a few more seconds before they lift to mine. "Being competitive is good. It can be bad, but it can also be good."

"Are you?"

He thinks for a bit. "I don't know. I guess I can be. Do you want to rest your hand for a few minutes?"

"Okay. Thanks." I sit down on one of the chairs.

"Would you like a drink?" He nods to the soda machines at the entrance of the bowling alley.

I wasn't thirsty, but now that he mentioned it, my throat feels drier than a desert. "Yes, please. Thanks."

He nods again before walking off. I push up my sleeve and examine my wrist. I don't see any bruises. Even though the pain is not as severe as before, it still hurts. I don't want this to ruin our game. I'm having lots of fun, and I know he is, too. Even though we're still a bit awkward around each other. Maybe it's the atmosphere. All the other times we spent time together, we were in privacy. The bowling alley is so noisy and I sometimes have to speak loudly for him to hear me. I like when we were in a closed space.

Josh returns with two bottles of Coke and hands one to me.

That Special Someone

"Thanks." I uncap it and gulp some down.

"How's your hand?" he asks.

"Getting better."

He sits down in the seat next to me.

We both tip our bottles to our mouths and sip.

"I'm having fun," I tell him.

He gives me a genuine smile. "Me, too."

We're both quiet again.

I look down at my shoes. Then I look at his. I laugh.

"What?" he asks.

I shake my head. "Sorry. Just a funny thought I had." I stretch my foot toward his. "Your shoes. They're huge."

He looks at them. "They're not *that* huge."

"Compare them to mine."

"You have baby feet."

"Nu uh! You have giant feet."

He chuckles. I do, too.

He looks at his again. "I guess they are kind of huge." He shakes his foot. "They are a little big on me."

"So are mine. Maybe they're supposed to be."

He sits back on his chair. "Look at us, talking about bowling shoes."

"I know. We're so boring."

"Well, I can't argue that I'm boring, but you don't have a boring bone in your body."

I feel my cheeks warm up. "This conversation seems oddly familiar."

"Yeah. We've discussed this before. In my office."

I remember the conversation as if it happened a few hours ago. But I didn't expect him to remember it. I didn't think I was important enough for him to remember. But the fact that he does shows that...what? That he likes me? I mean, obviously he likes me or else we wouldn't be here, but does he like...*really* like me?

When I look at him, I find him staring at me. "What?" I ask, fear starting to enter my veins. Is my hair a mess? Did some of my nearly-non-existent makeup rub off?

He shakes his head. "Sorry. I'm just trying to figure you out. You seem to be in your own world a lot."

I stare down at my lap. "I guess so. Maybe that's because after my..." I straighten up, though I keep my eyes on my knees. "When my f-father...I um...what I mean to say is..."

"Dini, if you're not ready to talk about this, it's okay."

I nod. "Thanks. It's just that...well, I never got close

enough to a guy to talk about it. I don't talk about it with anyone. I know it makes my mom sad, and my siblings don't like discussing it because they want to live their lives happily without the weight of it dragging them down. Maybe because they have families, it's easy to push it aside. But not for me."

Dad was closest to me out of all his kids. I know it's not fair to say I've been hurt most by his leaving because we've *all* been hurt, but it does feel that way.

"When the time is right," Josh says. "I'd love to be the person you feel comfortable enough to talk to."

I slowly lift my eyes to his.

"Sorry, that was way too forward." He shakes his head and mutters under his breath, like he's scolding himself.

"No, it's okay. Thanks. And I hope to be the person you trust to talk to about your um…whatever you need to talk about. I mean, if you have something. I don't mean to claim you have issues or anything. I just mean that everyone has things they're dealing with and—"

"Don't worry about it, Dini," he says, his voice soft. "You don't have to try to be perfect around me. I want you to be yourself."

I tuck my hands underneath my thighs. "I didn't realize I'm

trying to be perfect. I guess because of all the rejections I got from guys, I want to make the best impression. And we are on a *date*, as opposed to being in your office."

He nods. "It does feel different. More pressure."

I nod.

We're quiet again.

I take another sip of my Coke, then say, "Let's continue the game?"

His eyes dip to my injured hand. "Is your wrist okay?"

I twist it around. It still hurts a little, but not enough to hold me back from bowling. "It is, thanks."

We continue to play, and it doesn't take long for the pain to disappear completely. Josh wins both games by a landslide.

Chapter Nineteen

After bowling, Josh and I eat at a small restaurant. The food is delicious, but the place is noisy and crowded. That doesn't seem to bother either of us, though. It's like everything around us fades away and it's just me and him. We're still a little awkward with each other, but we're starting to grow more comfortable.

I'm a little disappointed when we leave the restaurant and head to the car. I don't want the date to end. The ride home goes by too fast and before I can blink, I find us parked in front of my house.

Josh gives me a sweet smile before climbing out and running to the passenger side to open the door for me. I thank him. We walk to the front door of my house, side by side. He's really tall. I'm wearing flats because I don't like heels, and I feel so short. I wonder if we look cute together.

No. I will not think that. Even though we had an enjoyable afternoon, I won't allow myself to grow vulnerable. I can't risk my heart like this, not until I know Josh and I really do have a chance. I hope we do. I can definitely envision a life with him, but I don't let my mind wander to that because I don't want to get too attached. I know I need to be positive, but after all the rejection I got, I need to be realistic. Even if Josh and I seem perfect for each other and get along, there's a chance we may not work out. I don't want to end up with a broken heart.

When my thoughts end and I'm back to the real world, I realize that Josh is standing by the door and I'm a few feet away from him. I must have stopped walking and just stood there thinking.

"Sorry," I say as I step closer to him. "I was lost in my own world again."

"That's okay. I had a really good time," he says.

I feel all warm inside. "Me, too."

He inclines his head. "Good night, Dini."

"Good night, Josh."

I watch him walk back to his car and climb in. Right before he pulls out of the driveway, he waves. I wave, too. I watch the car until it's out of sight, then enter my house. After closing the door behind me, I lean back and stare at the ceiling. I feel a large grin crawl onto my face. The date starts to play in my head, from the moment he picked me up to the moment I watched him get into his car. A satisfied sigh escapes my lips.

"Adina! You're back."

I lower my gaze and find Mom standing before me. She moves closer, her eyes scanning my face, reading everything written on it. "You had a good time," she says. It's not a question.

"Mmm," I mumble, my eyes returning to the ceiling. The date starts to replay in my head.

With a laugh, Mom puts her arm around me and leads me into the kitchen. "Are you hungry?"

"I already ate," I murmur, remembering how kind Josh was when I hurt my hand. Is it weird to admit that I miss him already?

"Adina, I've never seen you like this." Mom takes my hands and we sit at the table. "Tell me how it went."

I do. When I'm done, she leans back, her mouth slightly ajar.

"What?" I ask.

"Even when you came home from good dates, you never looked this excited." She throws her arms around me and hugs me so tight I'm sure my spine will snap.

"Mom!" I cry.

"I've been waiting for this day for years."

I try to free myself, but her hold is too strong. "I'm not engaged yet!"

"I know." She kisses my temple, not loosening her hold. "It's nice to see the light back in your eyes." She kisses me again.

She finally releases me. I bite down on my bottom lip. "I'm even more scared."

She tucks some hair behind my ear. "Why?"

"When I had a bad date, I didn't have to worry about getting hurt. And when I came back from a good date and then got rejected, it stung but not that much because while I liked the guy, I didn't...you know, *like* him. But with Josh—I mean, Yehoshua...."

"You have strong feelings for him."

I nod. "It's different because I got to know him before we went out. W-what if he realizes how weird I am and rejects me? It'll hurt. A lot."

That Special Someone

Mom scoots her chair closer to me and rubs my back. "You're not weird, sweetie. If Josh is the right man for you, he will accept you and love you for who you are. And if he's not the right guy, you will keep looking until you find him. It's worth it to put yourself out there and open your heart, even if it could get broken. Because if you don't, you'll never find happiness."

I see the pain in her eyes. I know she's thinking about Dad.

"Mom, can I ask you something?"

"Of course, honey."

"How come you never dated after Dad left?"

Some girls in my class started a rumor that my mom didn't get remarried because my father left her without giving her a *get*, a Jewish divorce. Which was *not* true. I used to hope she'd never get remarried because I believed deep down that my father would return. Did Mom hope so, too?

Mom shifts in her seat, clearly uncomfortable.

"I'm sorry," I say. "You never like talking about him."

"I don't," she whispers.

"I don't want to bring up bad memories. No one in the family wants to talk about it. But I...I do."

Mom leans forward, resting her elbows on the table and

laying her head on them. "I know. I do want to talk to you. I don't want to break down."

"Don't be scared to cry in front of me, Mom. You've been so strong for us. But we're all grown now and you don't have to protect us anymore."

Mom turns her head toward me, and I see tears welling up in her eyes. She reaches for my hand and I slide it into hers. "You are a great girl, Adina. Thanks so much for everything. I do want to talk, but not now. Maybe one day soon."

I nod. I don't want to pressure her to open up when she's not ready. I just want her to know that I'm here for her.

She reaches into her pocket for a tissue and wipes her eyes. "Do you want me to find out information about the boy?"

I shake my head. "I want to get to know Yehoshua for myself without asking other people's opinions. If he's a good guy, I want to be the one to discover it." Not that I'll have much to discover because I already *know* he's a good guy.

She tucks some hair behind my ear again. "Okay. Whatever you feel is best."

I give my mom another hug before heading to my room. I kick off my shoes, take off my jewelry, dress into a robe, and pull my hair into a ponytail. I sit down at my computer to work on my programming. I just need to focus on something instead of thinking about Josh. I can't get so obsessed.

Oh, but I had such a great time! I can't wait to get to know him better. I can't wait until we're close enough to tell each other our innermost thoughts and secrets.

If we get to that point. I know I'm scared to get my heart broken, but Mom's right. I need to risk it if I want to find happiness. I don't want to lose Josh because I'm scared to get hurt.

Clearly working on my game is not occupying my mind. I reach for my phone to call Avigayil, but it starts to ring, startling me. When I glance at the screen, my heart thumps. It's Josh.

I just sit there, frozen, staring at the screen, my blood speeding through my veins. Then I shake my head. "Hello?" My voice is too formal and too shaky.

"Hey, Dini."

"Hey, Josh." Still formal. Ugh, why am I still so awkward and shy around him?

He's quiet. Did he hang up? No, I hear him breathing.

After a few more seconds, he says, "I just wanted to wish you a good night. I know I already said it when I dropped you off, but…" He doesn't finish the rest of his sentence.

"That's so sweet!" Oops, did I just say that out loud? "I mean, that's very kind of you."

He chuckles. "What are you doing?"

"Working. Or trying to."

"Oh, I'm disturbing you?"

"No!" I practically shout. "I just mean I can't concentrate on my work because—" I snap my mouth shut. *Because I can't stop thinking about you or the date.*

He's quiet, as though he's waiting for me to finish my sentence.

I clear my throat. "Never mind. What are you doing?"

"Nothing, really."

Silence.

"I know I'm not supposed to contact you right after the date," he says. "Something about letting a few days pass so I don't seem too eager or whatever. But I don't care. I want to see you again."

My phone almost slips out of my hand. He wants to see me again! "Me, too! I mean…" I clear my throat. "It would be an honor to see you again," I say in a nonchalant voice.

He laughs again.

That Special Someone

"How about tomorrow morning at Markus Accounting?" I say, then giggle.

"Oh, right! Oh my God, I totally forgot we'll see each other at work tomorrow." He laughs like he's embarrassed.

"I know I've only been working there for a few weeks. Nice to know I'm so memorable," I joke.

"You are," he tells me. "Much more memorable than the other girls."

I don't know what to say. The fact that he thinks more highly of me than the other girls makes me feel really good, but also bad. There's nothing great about me. Nothing at all.

"Sorry," he says at my silence. "I'll, um…I'll see you tomorrow then?"

Did I offend him? I'm about to tell him that he doesn't have to hang up but what if he *wants* to hang up? He did call me after all, but what if this conversation confirms to him that I'm not the right girl for him? But he did just say I'm more memorable. Oh my Gosh, my head seriously needs to shut up.

"Dini?"

"Sorry. Lost in my own world again. Yeah, I'll see you tomorrow morning."

I feel him grin through the phone, if that's even possible.

"Good night, Shrimpi."

"*What?*"

"You're so short," he says. "Shrimpi."

"Shrimp? As in non-kosher sea food?"

He chuckles softly. "Yes, exactly."

I narrow my eyes, as if narrowing them at him. "Fine. *Lobster.*"

Now he says, "*What?*"

"Well if I'm a shrimp because I'm so short, then you're a lobster because you're so *tall.*"

A few silent seconds pass before he bursts out laughing. "Touché. Well played, Shrimpi. Well played."

My cheeks hurt due to the large smile capturing my face. "Why thank you, Lobster."

He laughs again. "Good night, Dini."

"'Night, Josh."

Chapter Twenty

The weather is beautiful. The birds are chirping, the air smells fresh, there are no conflicts in the streets, and the city bus is nearly-empty. Life is amazing.

Okay, I'm in a really good mood. How can I not be? I've never felt this way about a guy before. I've always dreamed I would one day, but as the weeks, months, and years went on, I knew my dream was fading away, little by little until it would poof completely. I worried I would settle for someone and not feel...*this*. But maybe God has finally answered my prayers. Maybe in just a few more months, I will no longer be single.

Oh, gosh. Is that *really* going to happen to me? I can't imagine it.

I find myself humming as I shrug out of my jacket and hang it in the office closet. Miriam walks over to me and bumps her hip into mine. "I'm guessing you had another good date?" she says with a knowing look in her eyes.

My cheeks warm up.

She sighs contently as her eyes get a faraway look. "I remember those days."

The other girls settle down at their desks, and Miriam and I do, too. My hands are a little clammy as I work on the bank statements. When's Josh going to come? I want to see him again. I want to talk to him again. See his soft eyes and sweet smile.

When the door *does* open, I feel butterflies enter my stomach. He's here. He strides in, his eyes automatically seeking mine. Our gazes lock, and time stands still. It's just me and Lobster, not saying anything with our mouths, but our eyes say enough. It's not until someone uses the stapler that we're yanked out of our...whatever. Josh's head snaps toward the direction of his office, and he heads there, but not before giving me a quick smile.

When I glance at my coworkers, I find each one of them eyeing me curiously.

I focus my attention on my papers, trying to hold back a blush. But I don't think it's possible to do that.

That Special Someone

Just when I think this will pass, Miriam rolls over. "Hey, Adina? Is there something going on between you and Yehoshua?"

I keep my eyes on my work for a few seconds before raising my gaze to Naomi. Just like I expect, she has jealousy and pain brewing in her eyes. I look down at the papers on my desk. I can't lie to Miriam, but I can't tell her the truth, either. I don't want to hurt Naomi, and I don't know if Josh wants to keep this a secret. I mean, not that we have anything to hide, but do we want the whole office to be in our business? Miriam is the type of person to pry and pry until she gets answers, and I can never say no to someone who begs so much. I'll crack like an egg.

Having this between Josh and me feels special. Sacred. I don't want anyone or anything to ruin it.

"Um...I'd rather not talk about it," I mumble. Raising my eyes to Naomi again, I see daggers in hers.

"Oh my gosh," Miriam half-yells, half-whispers. "Are you *dating* him? He's the one who's put you in such a good mood?"

"Miriam—"

"You two have been spending so much time together, and I know he looks at you in a certain way, you know? Oh my gosh!"

"Miriam, please."

"You'll only end up hurt," Naomi says, jutting out her chin. "Yehoshua is a heart breaker."

"Naomi," Faigy says.

"What? It's true. Just look at what he did to Suri."

"He feels really bad about the whole thing," I find myself saying. Shoot, I should have just kept quiet. It looks like weapons of mass destruction have been added to Naomi's eyes.

"So you talked about Suri with him," she says. "That was nice of you."

The room is dead quiet. Can Josh hear this from his office?

I want to defend him so badly, but I know that whatever I say will fall on deaf ears. Naomi will never respect my words. The best thing to do is to ignore her. I focus on my work.

Miriam rolls closer to me. "Adina."

"What?" I ask, trying to keep my voice patient, but I think I snapped at her.

She looks hurt for a second, but then she says, "Just be careful. I told you he's difficult. I mean, he's a good guy, but he's not the greatest when it comes to girls."

I want to tell her that out of all the guys I've dated, Josh

That Special Someone

Markus has been the kindest to me. But what if I'm missing something here? They've known him longer than I have. Could it be he's putting up an act and is really not a good person? The thought makes my heart tear a little. I like him a lot. I've never felt this way about anyone.

"I'm not saying you shouldn't give him a chance," she continues. "For all I know, he might be the perfect guy for you. But you're my friend, and I don't want you to get hurt."

I nod as my throat tightens. "Thanks."

Slowly, everyone gets back to work. I try to block out their words, but I can't just shove them aside. I need to know if Josh is a bad person. But am I one to listen to gossip? I firmly believe in giving people a chance. So many guys have rejected me and they could have easily told their friends how clumsy and awkward I am. They could have easily told them to steer clear of the weirdo. I don't want to do the same to Josh. These girls don't know him like I do, do they?

I'm so confused.

Mr. Markus arrives, and a few hours later, his son peeks his head into the room and asks if I'm ready to work on Greene. As I get up from my desk, I see the other girls eyeing me. I swallow a few times before entering his office.

His entire face lights up and he gives me such a sweet smile. "Hey, Shrimpi."

Some of my doubts fly out the window, and I return the smile, though mine is probably not as exuberant. "Hey, Lobster." I sit down.

"I find that I like 'Lobster' very much."

I smile, my lips shaking a bit.

His face falls. "What's wrong?"

I quickly shake my head. "Nothing."

He frowns, some pain entering his eyes. "You don't believe them…do you?"

My mouth turns dry. "You heard."

He nods curtly.

"Sorry! That was so rude to talk about you like that." I wring my hands in my lap, not knowing what to say. My mind is one big jumbled mess.

He plucks a pen off his desk and starts clicking it, his eyes on his keyboard. "I, um…" His voice is so low I almost don't hear him. I lean forward. "No one understands," he murmurs.

"What?"

He shakes his head. "I mean, no one understands me."

"I do," I say. At least, I think I do. There's still so much I don't know about him, like why he doesn't like bringing up his singing. But I feel like I do understand him.

"The other girls," he says, still not looking at me. "They think I'm a jerk."

"Because of Suri?"

He half nods. "I guess. Other things, too. They think I'm lazy and entitled because my dad's the boss. And they were all such great friends with Suri. Of course they'd sympathize with her and think of me as the bad guy. I don't blame them. And there's Naomi..." He sighs. Then he slowly lifts his eyes to me. "I'm looking for someone...different. Someone special."

Something gets stuck in my throat and my heart speeds up. Does he mean someone like me?

"I'm looking for someone special, too," I say.

He drops the pen and gathers Greene's papers that are on his desk. "You can tell them we're going out if you want." He's not looking at me again. "I'm so sick of caring what other people think. I just want to be happy."

"Me, too."

He raises his eyes to meet mine. And he gives me a warm smile.

***

After supper, I drive to Avigayil's house. I didn't have a chance to talk to her last night, and I really need to unburden myself. I feel comfortable talking to Mom, but I don't want to worry her with my dating woes.

Avigayil and I sit on her porch with potato chips. After discussing what's going on in our other friends' lives and things going on in the community, we get to the meat of things—dating.

"You first," I tell her.

"Okay. There's not much to tell, though. Shmuli and I have gone out on a few more dates. Things are going well, thank God." She blushes so red I wonder if her cheeks will ever regain their natural color.

I hug her. "I'm so happy to hear that!"

"Thanks. Now your turn."

"Um…" I play with my hair. "Yehoshua and I went on a date last night."

"What?!" She yells so loud it echoes down the street. She covers her mouth and giggles. "When did this happen? Last I heard, you and him had some sort of argument or something?"

"That's in the past."

"So how was it?" She's nearly bouncing in her seat.

That Special Someone

"The best date I've ever had in my life." And I tell her how my night went, as detailed as possible.

She squeals. "Maybe we'll get engaged around the same time! Oh my gosh, it'll be so much fun to go through it together." Her mouth closes when she sees me frowning. "What? I thought you said the date went well."

"It did. But my coworkers basically told me that I'll end up with my heart broken." I tell her what they told me. "Do you think I should listen to them? I mean, they don't know him like I do, but I don't want to end up with a bad guy, you know…"

"You said he was kind to you, right? That he was so considerate and caring when you hurt yourself?"

I nod.

"If he was a bad person, you'd know. You're smart, Adina. You have to listen to your instincts. Your coworkers may know him for longer, but that doesn't mean they *know* him."

"Yeah, that's what I was thinking. I don't want them to cloud my judgment. I know some people wouldn't say the greatest things about me. I don't want to write Josh off because of them. Not when he could be the guy I've been waiting for."

She encloses me in her arms. "Trust yourself. If he makes you feel good, then you have nothing to worry about. But if he ever makes you feel bad, you should think things over and figure out if he really is the right guy for you."

"Thanks," I tell her. "For everything."

"No problem."

Chapter Twenty-One

"A teensy weensy hint?" I ask Josh as he drives.

He shakes his head. "I want you to be surprised."

We left right after work. I don't mind that I'm not dressed up and that my hair might be a bit disheveled, and my makeup? Forget about it. All that matters is that I'm with Josh, and I'm very excited for what he has planned.

"I told my dad," he says. "About us."

"What did he say?" I ask, not sure I want to hear the answer. I'm pretty sure he's worried because of what happened with his last employee.

"He's happy for us," Josh says.

I sigh in relief. "Good, though it's going to feel…awkward."

"Why?"

"I don't know. I guess whenever I talk to him, I'll feel like he's studying me closely, trying to figure out if I'm a good match for you."

"Don't worry about it. He told me after the first week that he's pleased with you, that you're one of the most intelligent employees he's ever had."

"He did *not* say that."

He nods vehemently. "I promise he did."

I lower my head as I feel an intense blush take over. "Thanks."

When I raise my head, I see we're slowing down in front of the beach. Josh glances at me and smiles when he sees my shocked expression. "Surprise."

"The beach," I say dumbly.

"Yep."

"I love the beach! I love watching the water."

He grins. "I know."

We get out and he pops open the trunk, revealing what's inside. "A picnic basket," I say with the same shocked tone. We're going to have a picnic on the beach? That's so romantic. "When did you plan this?" I ask. He asked me if I wanted to go out with him only a few hours before the work day ended.

That Special Someone

He reaches for the basket, shuts the trunk, and leads me into the beach. "After you left my office," he says. "I wanted to do something special."

"That's why you randomly rushed out," I say. "To get everything ready."

He nods.

All for me. Every cell in my body warms with elation.

As we walk, I trip over the sand and head straight for the basket in Josh's arms. He manages to turn his body in time so I knock into his shoulder instead. "Sorry!" he says, lowering the basket and stepping closer to me. "Did I hurt you? It was just instinct to turn."

"It's okay. You saved the basket." I laugh lamely. "I would have ruined everything."

He shakes his head. "You could never ruin anything." He picks up the basket and we continue walking, searching for an area on the beach that has the least amount of people so we can have some privacy.

"It doesn't get better the more comfortable I am," I say as Josh pulls a blanket out of the basket and lays it on the sand. "I think I'll be clumsy no matter what."

"I don't mind it." He sounds one hundred percent sincere.

I may not be less of a klutz as the days pass, but I definitely feel more confident in myself. That's all due to Josh. I never thought I would actually find a guy who would be okay with all my shortcomings.

We sit down on the blanket. "Can I look inside the basket?" I ask.

"Sure."

I open it and rummage through its contents. Caesar salad, sandwiches, dessert. And something in a container. It looks homemade. I take it out and raise an eyebrow at him.

"Oh, that's another surprise for you."

I stare at it. "It looks like potato salad. Oh my gosh! Is it *your* potato salad?"

He nods with a grin. "Everything else is store bought."

"I can't wait to taste it!"

His cheeks redden. "I can't wait for you to taste it, either."

We pour water over our hands to wash for the sandwiches, then bite into them. Mine is chicken cutlets with grilled onions, tomatoes, lettuce and an amazing sauce. The Caesar salad is really good, too.

The wind blows through my hair, but I don't feel cold. It feels nice. There's a lot of activity around us, little kids making sand castles or waddling in the water. It reminds me of when I was a kid and my family would come here practically every Sunday. We gave up a lot of things after my dad left.

Josh opens the container and pours half of the potato salad on a plate, handing it to me. He pours the second half on his plate. We dig in. My eyes close as I savor the delicious flavors. This is the best potato salad I've ever eaten in my life! "Mmm," I tell him, opening my eyes. I take forkful after forkful until my plate is clear. "So good!"

His cheeks grow redder. "Thanks. I'm so glad you like it."

"I need the recipe for this. Like *right now*."

He laughs again, his cheeks even redder. "I'll gladly give it to you. Though, I'd rather make it for you."

I go still. Does he mean…?

He coughs and looks inside the basket. He digs around, but I can tell he's not really looking for anything. He's just trying to keep himself busy. I focus on finishing my sandwich.

After a little while, the awkwardness disappears and we start talking about many different things. Childhood memories, our families, what life we'd like to have after we're married. I'm relieved to learn that he and I share the same values.

"I've been meaning to tell you that the chocolate cake I had at your house the other day was *so* good," he says. "Your mother said you made it."

"Yeah. Thanks." I feel all giddy that he liked my cake. I want to tell him that I'd like to make it for him more often, but I don't want a replay of what happened a few minutes ago.

When we're finished eating, we clean up. "Thanks so much for this," I tell him. "It was amazing."

"You're welcome."

We get up and start walking along the shore, continuing to talk about everything and nothing. The water is so beautiful, so peaceful. I can stay here for hours.

When it starts to get dark, we gather the basket and get in the car. Josh just sits there, his gaze locked on the steering wheel.

"Josh? You okay?"

He blinks a few times, then turns to me. "Can I show you something? I haven't shown it to anyone else."

A jolt of excitement surges through me. "Sure."

He slips his phone out of his pocket and plugs it into the car. Then he presses a few buttons. After a second or two, music starts to play, followed by a soft, masculine voice. I don't recognize the song—it's probably an original one—but the voice sounds familiar. Whoever the singer is, he has a lovely voice. I wrack my brain, trying to pinpoint where I heard it, and then I see the expression on Josh's face. Embarrassment mixed in with pride, and hope.

"It's you," I say. "You're singing."

He nods. "It's a song I composed with my band. Do you like it?"

"I love it, Josh. You have such a beautiful voice."

He lowers his head. "Thanks."

"I didn't know you have a band. Do you want to sing professionally?"

He stares straight ahead, placing his hands on the steering wheel. "I would like to, but I don't know if it would work out. It seems so unrealistic. I need to focus on my job at the firm. Maybe one day."

"I hope you can fulfil your dream."

He nods and looks at me. "Thanks. You're such an inspiration to me. You're so passionate about your programming. You don't let anything get in your way. I really admire that."

My mouth moves, but no sound comes out. He *admires* me. When I find my voice, I say, "But I'm not really—I mean, I'm not so on top of it. I could push myself to try harder, I guess."

He shakes his head. "That doesn't matter. You don't give up, because you love it."

"Yeah. I do."

He focuses back on the spot in front of him. "When my parents first got married, they were extremely poor. My dad lost his job a few days after their wedding and my mom was in school. They had to save every last penny just so they could put food on the table. After hard work and determination, they managed to start a few successful businesses. Then they opened the firm and sold some of the businesses. My mom doesn't work with us anymore, but she used to, and my siblings have too, though I'm the only one there now. My parents don't want me to go through what they've been through, that's why they keep pushing me to stick with accounting. They pushed me to get a degree."

"That's understandable."

He nods. He detaches his phone and sits back in his seat.

"My dad walked out on us," I whisper. "I was ten."

He twists his head in my direction, his eyes filled with shock.

I nod. "He just got up and walked out. Though he did

manage to divorce my mom properly, thank God."

He just continues to stare at me in utter shock.

"That's why I have problems like…getting close to people. Especially men. I don't want to get hurt." I lower my gaze to my hands that are settled on my lap. "It was so hard the weeks following his leaving. I would stay home and only leave the house for school. I pushed away all my friends. I turned into a hermit. My social life went down the toilet. That might explain why I have issues in the social department. Programming was my anchor."

He reaches for me like he wants to hug me, but he drops his hands to his sides. "I'm so sorry, Dini. I didn't know."

I swallow the tears threatening to enter my eyes. "It's okay. I'm okay with it now." Which is a lie.

Based on his expression, I know he knows, too. "Did you ever think of tracking him down? Maybe there's a logical explanation."

I firmly shake my head. "If my dad wanted to reach out to us or have a relationship, he had lots of opportunities. He knows where we live. We're not the ones who disappeared." I shake my head again. "If he wanted to contact me, he would have. I don't want him to weigh me down anymore. I've shed too many tears over him. I need to forget about him and move on with my life."

Again, it looks like he wants to hug me, but he fists his hands. "I'm so sorry. I wish you didn't have to go through that."

My vision is blurry. If I blink, the tears will drip down my cheeks. I don't want to cry anymore.

He hands me a tissue. That makes me smile, which causes the tears to seep out of my eyes. I dab them. "Sorry," I say.

"Don't apologize," he says softly. "What you've been through is really hard. I can't imagine how you're feeling, but I want to be here for you."

"Thanks. I want to be here for you, too."

"Thanks, Dini the Shrimpi."

"What did you call me?"

"It's not such a perfect rhyme, but it's close."

"Dini the Shrimpi?"

"What? No like?"

I sit back and find myself giggling. "It's cute. Dini the Shrimpi...yeah, I like it!"

He has a satisfied smile.

"Then you're..." My eyebrows furrow. "Joshter the

That Special Someone

Lobster!"

The smile vanishes from his face. "Joshter the Lobster? Now that's pushing it."

"What? No like?" I tease.

"Joshter the Lobster," he says like he's rolling it around on his tongue. "Okay, I accept. Only because you came up with the name."

I laugh. "Dini the Shrimpi and Joshter the Lobster. We're *so* kosher." I start giggling like I've had too much to drink.

Josh starts laughing, too. My stomach hurts. He clutches his side.

Then he stops and looks at me. "I haven't laughed this much in a really long time. Thanks, Dini."

"I haven't, either. Thanks, Josh."

***

Mom walks into my room as I'm reading a romance novel. Yeah, a *romance* novel, not a thriller. Ever since I've been seeing Josh, I don't feel like I'm going to throw up when I open the page of a love story. The characters in the books get to have their happily ever afters, and maybe I can, too.

I slip my bookmark into the page and close it, giving Mom my full attention. She sits down on the corner of my bed.

"How was your day?"

"It was great." I don't think about work. I think back to the wonderful picnic I had with Josh, and to the sound of his beautiful voice. I'm so glad he shared it with me, and that I shared my story with him. I feel so close to him.

"I know you asked me not to, but I did research on the Markus boy," Mom says.

"Yehoshua, Mom." He means so much more to me than "The Markus Boy." He's my Josh. My Lobster. I laugh to myself at how ridiculous I sound. Then I frown. "Did you find out something bad?" Fear crawls into my organs and limbs.

She shakes her head. "On the contrary, I heard really good things about him and his family."

A relieved sigh leaves my mouth. "You scared me."

She strokes my hair. "I just worry about you, that's all."

"What are you worried about?"

"Since we're not doing this the traditional way, I feel uneasy. I don't have a problem with you meeting this guy on your own, I'm just not used to it. So I'm concerned."

"You don't have anything to be worried about, Mom. Josh is a good guy." He doesn't open up to people like he does with me, which is probably why my coworkers are hesitant about him. He was just looking for someone who'd understand him, just like I was.

"I don't want him to play around with you, Adina. I need to know he's serious. I can't bear seeing you hurt."

I shift over so I can hug her. "I'll be okay. Yehoshua is serious about me. He told his dad we're going out. You don't have to look after me anymore. I can take care of myself."

"I know, sweetie. It's just that you've always been a little more sensitive than your siblings."

She's referring to what happened with Dad, how I became basically nothing but an empty shell while my siblings seemed to move on with their lives. They were affected, of course, they just knew how to hide it.

I pull out of the hug. "I've never been this happy before. Please don't ruin it."

She quickly shakes her head. "Sorry, honey. I don't mean to ruin it. Just let me know if anything is bothering you, okay? I want you to know you can talk to me whenever you need to."

I nod. "I know. Thanks."

She puts her arm over my shoulder, pulling me close. Her lips press on my temple. "To answer your question, sweetie, I didn't date after your father left because looking out for myself was the last thing on my mind. I had five kids to raise all on my own. Your grandparents helped, but I had to be both mother and father. I had to push my kids' well-being before my own. My happiness didn't matter—yours did. I knew I had to focus all my energy on you and not occupy myself with dating. I needed to help all of you through it."

I lay my head on her shoulder. "Thanks for telling me. Did you think he would come back?"

"I hoped, Adina. I prayed he would. I begged Hashem to send him back so we could be a happy family again."

"We're okay," I tell her. "You did a phenomenal job."

She kisses the top of my head. "Thanks."

Chapter Twenty-Two

Josh and I have been going out for two weeks. We're more open with each other, and I feel like I can trust him. Many of my coworkers have claimed that Josh seems to be a different person. He used to stay in his office without exchanging more than a few words with anyone, but he seems more social now. Happier. I'm not a miracle worker, but just like me, Josh has been searching a very long time for his special someone. He told me he's never felt this way about anyone, just like me.

We're dating seriously now. I know he's the one. He's the guy I've been looking for these past five years.

We don't really talk much at work because of the way everyone watches us. Even Mr. Markus, who wears a large grin on his face whenever he sees me. I can't help but feel embarrassed. He might be my father-in-law. Oh my gosh, I can't believe I'm actually thinking about this.

Even Naomi seems to be okay with it. She still gives me dirty looks, but her eyes are not as hard as before. Michal told me that she's going out with a guy, so I guess that's the reason she seems okay with Josh and me. I hope things work out between them.

Miriam comes out of the bathroom and face plants on her desk. "This nausea is killing me," she moans. "Being pregnant is no fun."

I rub her back. "Sorry. But in just a few months, you'll have a baby!"

Her entire face lights up. "God willing."

"God willing."

My phone beeps. It's a text from Josh.

Hey, Shrimpi. Can you please come to my office?

I practically leap to my feet. Miriam raises her head and her eyes fill with humor. "Did someone special just text you to come see him?"

I playfully punch her shoulder, though not too hard because she's not feeling well.

"Just make sure to invite me to your engagement party!" she calls as I'm heading to Josh's office. The rest of the girls chuckle.

I knock on the door before pulling it open. Josh's face lights up like it always does when he sees me. "Dini the Shrimpi has arrived."

"To Joshter the Lobster's office," I say.

We both laugh.

"Here, sit down. I want to show you something."

I lower myself in my usual seat in front of his desk. He comes over to sit in the chair next to me. He's holding a manila envelope. Is that another project we're going to work on?

He clutches it to his chest. "How's work going?" he asks.

"Fine," I say, a little confused as to why he's asking me that question. Today's work is the same as any other day.

"You're not having problems with anything? The filing is going okay?"

I raise my eyebrows. "Yeah. The file cabinet is still the same. It hasn't fallen into some vortex that switched all the files around..."

He laughs sheepishly. "Yeah. Of course."

He's nervous. About what? Does it have something to do with the envelope? Oh my gosh, he's nervous! Does that mean he's about to ask me a very serious question? But he wouldn't do that at work, would he? It would be a bit weird. I mean, this is the place we met, but…and I doubt he'd hide a diamond ring in a manila envelope.

He stares at his desk, his hand on the envelope that's still pressed to his chest. I'm bursting to ask him what's going on, but it's obvious he's stressing out about whatever he wants to tell me. I tuck my hands underneath my thighs and wait patiently.

After what feels like hours but is probably only a few minutes, Josh scoots his chair closer to the desk and lowers the envelope on it. I watch curiously as he unwinds the string and sticks his hand in. He doesn't pull the papers out, though. He just leaves his hand in there.

"Dini," he says, looking at me.

I nod expectantly.

"After you told me about your dad, I couldn't stop thinking about him. I felt so bad for what you went through and what you're still going through. So I hired a private investigator to track him down."

I feel my eyes nearly pop out of their sockets. "You *what?*"

He pulls out the papers.

I put my hand on his and shove the papers back inside.

Then I realize my skin is touching his. I quickly pull my hand away. "Stop," I say.

He looks at me, and I can see the confusion in his eyes. "What's wrong?"

I shoot to my feet and grab hold of the sides of my head. "You hired a *private investigator*?"

"Yeah. To track down—"

"Why would you do that?"

He gets up and moves closer to me, but I step back. "Dini..."

"*Why would you do that?*"

He swallows hard. "I saw how hurt you were because he left you. I thought I could hire someone to track him down so that..."

"So that what? So that I could drop in on him for a family reunion?"

"I thought you'd be happy."

I squeeze the sides of my head again. "You spent your money on hiring a private investigator."

"I don't mind."

"But I do! We're not...we're not..." The words get struck in my throat. I force them out. "We're not married!"

"I never said we were."

"Who gave you permission to do this?"

"I was trying to help. I thought you would be happy."

"What did I tell you at the beach?" I say. "That if my dad wanted to be in my life, he would contact me. Did I not tell you that?"

He holds out his hands. "Shrimpi, please calm down."

"Calm down? How would you feel if a stranger hired someone to investigate one of the most private and traumatizing parts of your life?"

His whole face changes. "A stranger? That's all I am to you?"

Guilt eats away at my insides. I didn't mean to call him that. He's not a stranger, not at all. But that's way off topic. "You had no right, Yehoshua. *No right.*"

"So now I'm Yehoshua."

"Stop making this about you!" I nearly shout.

He looks like I slapped him across the face. "You're right. I'm sorry."

I fall down on the chair and bury my face in my hands, sobbing. This feels like such an invasion of privacy. I didn't tell him about my father so that he could hire a stranger to "investigate." A stranger who would dig into my life and my dad's life. If I marry him, would he do things like this without asking me?

I hear him sit down near me. "Don't cry, Dini. I'm sorry I hurt you."

I wipe my eyes with my sleeve. "I—I need to go." I need to be alone and make sense of my thoughts.

"Okay," he says unsurely.

I stand up and march out the door. But instead of going to my desk, I lock myself in the bathroom and wash my face, hoping to erase any evidence that I've been crying. Once I get to my desk, I see the girls looking at me, though trying not to be obvious about it. They must have heard us. For some reason, that causes fresh tears to pool in my eyes. I gather my bag and leave the office.

I walk and walk, not knowing where I'm headed. My head clouds with what happened in Josh's office. Did I overreact? I know he was just trying to help, that he had no malicious intent. He honestly thought he was helping me. But I feel so…violated. Betrayed.

I find myself in the park. Dropping down on one of the benches, I hug myself tight. I didn't take my jacket with me and it's a little chilly. The tears I've been battling since I left the office rush down my cheeks.

I overreacted. I shouldn't have yelled at him like that. I feel horrible for hurting him.

Yet, he had no right to go behind my back and hire a stranger to dig into my life. Why couldn't he have spoken to me about it first? I thought we were open with each other.

I remain in the park for half an hour, until I calm down. When I return to the office, it's dead quiet. Josh's door is closed. I want to go in and apologize, but I think we both need a break to think things through. I don't want to yell at him again. I don't want to hurt him any more than I already have.

When I get to my desk, I see the manila envelope sitting there with a Post-it note on top. **You might not want this now, but you might change your mind in the future. I want you to have it. -J.**

I dump it in my bag, out of sight. I'll throw it out when I leave today. No, I know I won't do that. I'll keep it, just in case one day I'll be brave enough to open it.

Keeping my focus on my work helps somewhat. The conversation I had with Josh still plays in my head from time to time, but I force it away and concentrate on my documents.

That Special Someone

Miriam tries to strike a conversation with me a few times, probably wanting to know what happened in Josh's office, but I tell her I'm busy.

The day comes to an end, but I still have a lot of work to do. I'll have to stay another few minutes.

Miriam puts her things away, then comes over to me. "You okay, Adina?"

"I'm fine."

She touches my shoulder. "Okay."

The other girls look at me, some giving me sympathetic smiles. Even Naomi looks somewhat sorry for me, though I'm pretty sure I see a glint in her eye. I ignore them and focus on my work. I want to get out of here as fast as possible. As much as I want to talk to Josh, I'm terrified. What if I messed everything up because I overreacted? What if he thinks I'm some unstable, crazy girl and he'll run for the hills?

Just as I'm finishing up my work, I hear yelling from Mr. Markus's office. It's Josh and his dad.

Like the last time, I can't hear what they're saying, but they both sound pretty riled up. I'm about to pack up and leave, but Mr. Markus's door springs open and he marches out. He doesn't look my way, just slams the door after him.

Chaya T. Hirsch

The office is silent.

I get up from my desk and head for Mr. Markus's office. Josh is standing by the window, his shoulders heaving. "Josh," I say.

He whirls around to face me. Then he turns back to the window. His shoulders still heave.

"What's going on?" I ask. "You okay?"

When he doesn't answer, I take a few hesitant steps inside. He still doesn't look at me.

"Do you want me to leave?" I ask, taking a few more steps inside. "Because I will if you want me to."

"No, don't leave."

I move closer, until I'm right next to him.

His back is still facing me. He rakes his hands through his hair. "I messed up."

"What do you mean?"

"The reason I don't like talking about my singing is because it reminds me of all the heartache and stress I brought my parents. As much as I love it, I hate it, too."

I just stare at his back, not understanding what he's telling me.

He slowly turns around. There are no tears in his eyes, but

278

they are filled with so much pain that my heart hurts for him.

"I want to hear the whole story, Josh," I say. "Please."

He nods, swallowing hard. "A few years ago, my band and I were performing at my niece's birthday party. We were approached by a man. He offered to sign us. I was so excited. My whole band was excited. My dad wasn't so sure about it. He tried to talk me out of it because he didn't have a very good feeling about it because the man was asking us to pay a significant amount of money, claiming we'd earn it back within a day. But I was so excited and I didn't want to listen to my dad. When he refused to pay, I used my own money. My bandmates chipped in, too, but it was mostly my money because they were broke. I was pretty broke myself and used up all my savings. I was so sure we were going to be the next big thing in Jewish music."

My heart pounds in my head. I know this story is going to take a turn for the worst, and I'm nervous for what I'm about to hear.

"He scammed us," Josh says, his hands fisting at his sides. "He kept asking for more money, telling us not to worry because we'd make it back. I dipped into the money saved aside for my college tuition. I asked my father for a loan. I didn't realize our so-called 'producer' owed a lot of people money. He signed my name, so I was the one liable for the payments. It turned out we owed people lots of money." He turns to the window again. "My dad bailed me out of some of the debt, but we still owe a lot of people money."

"I'm so sorry, Josh."

"A few days ago, a friend of mine told me about this guy who might be interested in signing us. My dad refuses to hear it. He's scared we'll get scammed again. He doesn't trust anyone in the music business. But if this guy is legit and we sell, we can pay off all our debt. That's what we keep arguing about. I feel so good about it, but I don't want to put my parents through this again."

I walk around him to stand next to him by the window. "I'm sorry for all that's happened to you. It sucks."

He lightly laughs. "Yeah." He turns his head to me. "I love music so much. All I want is to perform. I don't know what to do."

I wish I knew what to say to comfort him, but my mind turns blank. Maybe he doesn't need me to say anything. Maybe it's enough that I just be here with him. That I'm here to listen.

We stand quietly next to each other, staring out the

window. I've always found looking out the window peaceful. It's the perfect way to make sense of my thoughts. I feel so bad for what Josh has been through. And all the money he and his family have lost because of this. That guy is such a jerk for doing this to them.

I step back when a sudden thought hits me. "Josh…"

He looks up.

"Your family is in debt. You're in debt."

He nods, his eyes still filled with pain.

"You hired that private investigator. That must have cost you a fortune."

"Don't worry about it. I wanted to do it for you."

"No. Don't tell me not to worry about it. You know that you're in debt. You know that your parents are helping you pay back all those people. Yet you went ahead and hired a private investigator."

"Please don't get upset, Dini. I wanted to do it for you."

"Why would you do that?" I ask, trying to keep my cool. "It was such a reckless and impulsive thing to do."

"Dini—"

"How am I supposed to feel?" I ask, holding back a fresh batch of tears. "That you spent all that money on me? That you pushed me in front of your family?"

His gaze drops to his shoes. "I really like you and want to make you happy."

I step back, holding my hands up. "This is too much."

"I'm sorry," he says, moving closer as I move back. "I honestly thought you would want me to find your dad."

I shake my head vigorously. "No. You should have asked me before doing something this profound. I can't believe you would cause yourself and your parents to have an even bigger debt."

"Dini…"

"No." I march to the door and yank it open. "I need to be alone. Please don't follow me."

Chapter Twenty-Three

I'm sitting on my bed with my legs pressed to my chest, replaying what happened in Mr. Markus's office. I don't know what to make of it. First of all, he went behind my back and hired a stranger to dig into my life. That's such an invasion of privacy. I know he apologized, which is why it's easy to forgive him. But I don't know if I can forgive him for spending money to hire the investigator.

It shows that he's sweet, that he cares about me. But to put his family in even more jeopardy? Can I have a future with someone like that? I never asked him to find someone to track down my father. That's what bothers me the most. All he had to do was talk to me. And after I specifically told him I don't want to search for him, he went behind my back. Why?

Josh called me a few times and sent me some texts, but I

didn't respond to any of them. I don't know what to say to him. I don't want to answer until I know exactly how I feel, because I don't want to say the wrong thing.

I lean my head back and rub my hand down my face. I guess I don't understand him as well as I thought.

Mom peeks her head inside. "Hey, honey." She scrutinizes me. "What's wrong?"

"I don't know."

She sits down next to me. "Care to share what you're feeling?"

I puff out some air. "Let's say someone did something for you, something you didn't want him to do. Something that actually hurts you, but he thought he did it for your benefit. Then you find out other people got hurt because of this thing he did. The thing you didn't want him to do in the first place."

Mom's forehead wrinkles. She thinks for a few seconds. "People are always going to be doing things for you, even things you don't want or need. But if he keeps doing it and it gets overbearing, maybe the best thing is to break things off with him."

She knows I'm talking about Josh. I don't want to tell her details, though. I don't want to speak ill about him.

That Special Someone

"I'm just so confused, Mom."

She caresses my cheek. "Talk to him, Adina. The most important thing in a relationship is communication. Tell him how you feel. If the two of you are not on the same page, maybe the best thing for you to do is go your separate ways."

Mom's right. The only way to get through this is to talk it out with Josh. He tried at the office, but I just blew up on him. But he needs to understand that he can't go behind my back and do these things. He's hurting me more than helping me. I need to pay him back for the money he spent on that investigator. I know he'll put up a fight, but I won't give up.

But besides the money, we really do need to talk. I'm too tired, and I honestly don't want to deal with it right now. I'll have to have a talk with him tomorrow. If he refuses to understand that he can't do this sort of thing again, maybe we do need to go our separate ways. The thought makes my heart feel like it's splitting in half. I like him so, so much. I've never been so happy before. But if this goes on for longer, I won't be happy anymore.

I just hope he's willing to work it out.

***

Josh hasn't arrived yet. I try to focus on my work, but it's not easy. I want to talk to him already. I want to know that we're okay, that we're both willing to make this work.

Two hours pass. No Josh.

Four hours pass. No Josh.

I take my lunch. No Josh.

When it's 2 PM, I conclude that he's not coming in today.

Is it because of me? I chew on my thumbnail, something I haven't done in years, something I only do when I'm extremely worried.

Maybe he needs a break. But does that mean he doesn't want to work things through?

I take out my phone and compose a text. **Hey, Josh. Can we talk tonight?**

I focus on work as I wait for his response to come. It doesn't.

The day is over. I pack up along with everyone else, but I'm moving on autopilot. Is Josh avoiding me? I know I walked out on him yesterday and told him not to follow me. I hope he didn't think I wanted to break things off.

As I'm heading for the city bus, I call him. It rings and rings until I get his voicemail. I leave him a quick message, asking him to call me back.

That Special Someone

A part of me worries he never will.

***

It's been three days. Josh hasn't stepped foot in the office.

I'm beyond concerned at this point. I've called and texted him countless times and have received no response. I don't understand why he won't come to work. It can't be because of me, can it? Is it possible he thought we broke up and decided to quit so I wouldn't have to? So I wouldn't have to go through what Suri did? Why wouldn't he just answer his phone so I can explain that I don't want to break up? It's like he disappeared off the face of the planet.

Knowing I can't wait a second longer, I head to Mr. Markus's office. I wanted to talk to him yesterday, but I told myself to give Josh one more day. Maybe he needed time. Maybe he was sick. I didn't want to blow things out of proportion. But now that three days have passed, I know something is up.

Mr. Markus smiles when I walk in, though I can tell it's strained. "Adina! Please, sit down."

I do.

"What can I do for you today?"

I gnaw on my bottom lip. "Is Yehoshua feeing okay? He

287

hasn't been in for a few days."

The expression on my boss's face tells me he's not surprised I asked about his son. He leans back in his chair and sighs. "Yehoshua won't be working here anymore."

My blood turns cold. "What? Why?"

His eyes look apologetic. "Adina, you're a very nice girl. Please, forget Yehoshua and meet a nice boy."

My heart is thumping in my head, creating a whooshing sound. So many questions buzz around in my mind, but my throat is too dry. I just sit there, staring at him with what is most likely the most dumbfounded look on my face. Is he saying…Josh ended things with me?

Mr. Markus's eyes still look apologetic. He doesn't ask me to leave. He just sits there patiently, probably waiting for me to make peace with the news I just heard.

I bite hard on my bottom lip, forcing the tears to stay behind my eyes. "Why?" I manage to croak. *What about me?*

"Adina," he says softly. "I tried to talk him out of leaving, out of leaving you. But his mind is made up. He's not even living in Brooklyn anymore. The best thing for you to do is forget about him and find a nice boy to marry. Yearning after him will only get you hurt."

That Special Someone

But...but...

"If I can talk to him," I say.

Mr. Markus shakes his head. "I don't think that will do any good. He told me explicitly that..." His face fills with guilt.

"That what?" I ask.

"That he doesn't want to see you again."

It can't be true. It just can't be. Just three days ago, he told me how much he liked me, that it was due to how he felt about me that he hired that investigator to track down my dad. And now, all of the sudden, he doesn't like me anymore?

It's all my fault. I pushed him away. The one guy I actually thought I could have a future with.

The tears start to rebel, but I shove them away. There's so much I want to ask Mr. Markus. *Are you sure? Maybe he's just hurt? Maybe he needs time? If I can talk to him, maybe he'll reconsider and give us another chance?* But he made it clear that Josh has made his decision. And considering he hasn't answered my calls and texts for the past three days, it's obvious he wants nothing to do with me.

"Thanks," I say in a grave voice.

He nods, still looking apologetic.

I stand up and walk back to my desk in a daze. We're over.

I can't believe we're over. Just last week, I thought he'd be my husband. I dreamed of what our life would be like together. And now…

Miriam rolls over. "I heard you talking about Yehoshua in Mr. Markus's office. What's going on?"

Keep the tears at bay. Keep the tears at bay.

I open my mouth, only to find it shaking. I wait a few seconds before trying again. "He's not going to work here anymore."

"What? I guess it's not so surprising, since he works here on and off." She touches my arm. "Are you okay? I mean, are you guys still going out?"

I shake my head.

She hugs me, but I'm as stiff as a board. I just sit still in my seat.

"Adina," she says when she pulls away.

"I'm fine," I mutter. "We weren't that serious." Total lie.

She appears doubtful, but she nods, gives my arm a squeeze, and then gets back to work.

I don't know how I keep the tears from exploding out of my eyes, but I do. It's not until I'm alone in my room that I break down.

Chapter Twenty-Four

The last time I cried this hard was the day my father left.

I've been through many things since then, the ups and downs of life, like anyone, but these two incidents have made me feel like my heart is bleeding. Maybe that's extreme, maybe I'm being overdramatic, but I feel so... *bad*.

He won't even let me explain. He just cut me out of his life. That means he doesn't want to make us work. He has no interest in having a future with me. Is it all my fault, or was this doomed to happen no matter what? Maybe I'm doomed to be single for the rest of my life. It took me five years to meet a guy who seemed to accept me for who I am. Will it take me another five to find someone else? No, I don't want to find someone else. I want Josh. My Lobster.

I roll over to the other side of my bed and squeeze a pillow to my chest. I've been crying for a few hours. The tears don't dry up. It amazes me how there's a never-ending fountain behind my eyes. They say crying makes you feel better, and it has proven true in the past, but not now.

The door to my room creaks open. "Adina?" Mom whispers, "are you sleeping?" She moves closer and must see my tear-splattered cheeks, because a small gasp leaves her mouth. "Sweetie, what's wrong?"

The bed sinks as she sits down near me. Her hand strokes my hair. I shut my eyes and hug the pillow tighter to my chest.

"It's Yehoshua," she says. It's not a question or a guess.

I nod.

I feel her lower her cheek to mine. It seems like she doesn't mind my wet face. "Oh, sweetie, what happened?"

Mom's comfort causes more tears to rush to my eyes. As much as she wants to help me, protect me, scare away the monsters of life, she can't. She can't shield me from getting my heart broken.

"He just left," I say, my throat scratchy from crying so much. "It's over. We're over."

Her hands come around me. She holds me, telling me I'm going to be okay, that everything is going to be okay. "You're strong," she says. "You'll get through this."

I'm transported to when I was ten years old, to when my mom held me in the same manner, telling me that we'll be okay. The next few years were hard, but I did manage to move on with my life. Sort of. I don't think that's the case here. I can't imagine moving on from this.

"You'll meet the right guy one day," she says, rocking me. "With God's help, you'll meet him. And you'll be so happy, you'll forget all about this."

"I don't want to meet someone else," I sob. "I want Josh Markus."

She continues rocking me. "I know it seems hard, that your heart will never heal from this, but it will. You have to believe me."

"How do you know?" I whisper.

"How else could I have survived after your father left?"

I shift over so that my arms come around her. "I don't know how you did it." I sob into her shoulder. "I feel like I'm going to die."

"It'll get better. I promise. I'll make you something to eat, okay?" She kisses my cheek.

Before she pulls away, I tighten my hold on her. "Thanks

for everything, Mom. I don't think I would be able to go through any of this without you."

She kisses the top of my head before leaving my room.

I lie in the same position, not moving just sniffing.

When my phone rings, I nearly jump to the ceiling. Josh is finally returning my call! I sit up and frantically search for it. It must have fallen somewhere. After what feels like forever, I see it on the floor. I sweep it up.

My heart sinks when I see the name flashing on the screen. It's not Josh.

"Hey, Avigayil," I say.

"Hi! How are you?"

"I'm okay." Lie.

She seems a bit more cheery than usual, or maybe it feels that way because I'm feeling so down.

"So guess what? I get a *mazel tov!*"

The wind gets knocked out of me. "You're...you're engaged?"

She squeals. "Yes!"

It feels like the walls of the room are closing in on me and I can't breathe. Avigayil is engaged. Engaged. When I just had my heart broken.

That Special Someone

I shake my head, telling myself to get rid of these selfish thoughts. I know how Avigayil struggled to find her soulmate. I've listened to her tears and heartache over the past few years. I should be happy for her. I *am* happy for her. But why does she get her happily ever after while I lie here with my heart shattered? I want to yell, *It's not fair!*

No man will ever love me. My dad walked out on me. Josh walked out on me. I'm destined to be alone and miserable for the rest of my life.

"Adina? You there?"

I take a deep breath, telling myself to relax. "*Mazel tov*, Avigayil! I'm so excited for you." I do mean it. Even though I'm jealous and hurt, I am sincerely happy for my friend.

"You'll never guess how he proposed," she says, telling me how he took her to the spot where they had their very first date and popped the question under the stars. "Soon you'll get engaged, and we'll go through it together. We'll get married at the same time and we'll have kids at the same time and our kids will be best friends just like their mommies."

Tears spill over my eyes and down my cheeks. I think I'm going to throw up.

"And of course our husbands will be best friends, too," she

continues.

"Hey, Avigayil?" I say, my voice shaking.

"Yeah?"

"You probably have tons of people to call. We'll talk later, okay?"

"Okay. I can't wait to tell you more! Bye."

I hang up, grab my pillow, clutch it tightly to my chest, and turn to my side, shutting my eyes. Shutting out the world and the feelings in my heart.

Chapter Twenty-Five

I call in sick the next morning. I don't have the will or energy to be among people.

Mom makes me breakfast before leaving for work. From the look in her eyes, I know she wishes she could do something to help me feel better. But we both know there's nothing she or anyone can do. I have to ride it out, wait days, weeks, months, maybe even years for my heart to not feel so empty.

I munch on my pancakes, trying to blot out the images of Josh's face from my mind. I don't want to see his tall frame, dark hair, soft eyes. I don't want to see the way his whole face lights up when he laughs. I don't want to see the warm look in his eyes when our gazes locked. I don't want to hear the words, "Dini," "Shrimpi", or "Lobster." I want my brain to erase every last memory of him.

Chaya T. Hirsch

Staying home alone will drive me insane. I reach for my phone and dial my sister Henny, asking if I can drop by and play with baby Penina. She seems surprised and asks why I'm not going to work. I tell her it's my day off.

After dressing into something—I don't pay attention what—I tie my messy hair into a ponytail. I get down on my knees and rummage in the bottom drawer of my dresser for THE ENVELOPE. The culprit responsible for my aching heart. I scan the front of it, seeing the words "Adina Reid" written in his handwriting.

I fall back and cross my legs, holding the envelope like there might be a bomb inside. I carefully lower it to the floor and stare at it. I don't want to know what's in there. Except, that's a lie. A major lie. Maybe the reason I blew up on Josh Markus was because I *do* want to know about my father. I *do* want to have a relationship with him. I'm just too scared to admit it.

I got upset at him for no reason. But maybe something good *could* come out of this. I just need to open my heart, risk getting hurt. Again.

It's been fifteen years. Maybe there doesn't need to be a sixteenth.

That Special Someone

I tuck the envelope into my bag and take the bus to Henny's house. She opens the door, holding the adorable Penina in her arms. I reach for the baby and snuggle her.

"What's going on?" Henny asks, closing the door and following me into the living room, where we sit on the couch.

"Nothing." I nuzzle Penina's nose, making her giggle. That brings a smile to my face. A real smile. Before my sister can press further, I say, "How's your back?"

"Much better. Turns out I just pulled a muscle."

"I'm glad to hear you're feeling better. How's it going with Dov?"

"It's going well." She grins. "He and I sat down the other day and I told him how I was feeling. We discussed many things, were open with one another, and I feel we got to an understanding. He told me how much he loves me and that he is very happily married. I guess I was just being insecure." She laughs like she's embarrassed. "Marriage is a lot of work, Adina. It's something you constantly have to work at, but it's so rewarding." She tickles Penina. "Isn't it, my darling?"

Penina giggles.

My chest feels heavy. I'm willing to put in the work. I want to make things work with Josh. I guess he doesn't feel the same. Maybe I have been blinded all this time. Maybe he isn't the right guy for me. Just because we got along and he seemed to accept me for who I am, that doesn't mean he's my soulmate. Maybe my special someone is still out there somewhere. If I let my heartbreak consume me, I may never meet him. But what if Josh *is* my soulmate?

Needing to occupy myself with something, I turn to my sister. "Henny, I'm going to ask you something serious."

"Uh oh," she jokes. "Adina is going to ask something serious? It must be a very big deal."

Normally I'd laugh, but I'm too nervous for what I'm about to ask and I'm too broken because of Josh. "Do you ever think about Dad?"

She looks at me like I asked her to help me cover up a crime. Her face is sheet white, her eyes and mouth are wide, and I see her breathing growing labored. But she recovers and says, "Why are you asking me that?"

I reach for my bag and take out THE ENVELOPE. "What if I told you I tracked him down?"

She gapes at it. "You *tracked* him down?"

"I wasn't the one who did," I say. "I mean…it doesn't matter. The point is that I have all the information here."

That Special Someone

Henny cups her hand around her forehead. She rubs it like she's getting a headache. "Why, Adina?" she asks. "Why would you drag all this back into our lives? We pulled ourselves out of it. I made a wonderful life for myself, and God willing when you meet the right one, you'll build a great life for yourself, too. We don't need this."

I swallow the lump in my throat. "You never think about him? You never think about possibly having a relationship with him?"

She closes her eyes, rubbing her forehead again. "Of course I do. But then I think back to the years after he left. How broken we all were. I heard Mom cry herself to sleep every night. I saw my little sister falling into a dark hole. I promised myself I'd never forgive him."

My fingers trace the envelope. "I'm not going to tell you how to feel or what to do. But I think I'm willing to at least open a window."

She releases a shaky breath. "It's up to you."

"I don't want to do it alone. Will you do it with me?" I lay the envelope on my lap.

She lowers her hand from her head and looks at me. I see tears in her eyes. She studies the envelope. "I…I don't know."

"Please, Henny. I'm so scared to do it alone."

Maybe if things were different, if Josh and I were still together, I would have him by my side and I wouldn't have to put my sister through it. But circumstances aren't so.

"I don't want to cause you any pain," I say. "I just feel like I need to do this."

She stares at the envelope for a little bit before nodding. "You're right. This is something we need to do. The both of us. I can't keep running away from the past. Sooner or later, I'll have to make peace with all that's happened."

"We don't have to do anything once we see what's inside here," I tell her. "But we might regret it if we don't."

She nods. "I'm ready."

After putting the baby in her playpen, I place the envelope between our laps and look at Henny. She nods. I unwind the string, take a deep breath, then pull out the papers. Both of us gasp when we see his photo. The man...he's my father. I mean, obviously he's my father, but he's my *dad*. He has gray hair and brown eyes, the same color as mine and Henny's, and a black yarmulke on his head. His features are so familiar, as though I just saw him a few hours ago. This is the man who taught me how to ride a bike, picked me up when I fell, and kissed my wounds. The man who was my hero until the day he walked out on me.

He's much older than I remember, which is expected.

Henny reaches into her pocket for a tissue and dabs her eyes. "I can't believe we're actually doing this."

I scan the papers. "He lives in Brooklyn. Not that far."

"So he's been living in Brooklyn all this time and never thought to drop by and see how we're doing?"

"I…I don't know," I say, continuing to study the text. "He's not married."

"So?"

"I thought he was for sure married and had a new family."

She leans forward to examine the papers. "You think that means something?"

"I don't know. Do you…" I take a deep breath and let it out slowly. "Do you want to go see him?"

She bites down on her bottom lip. "After all these years…"

"I don't want to wonder for the rest of my life. I have so many questions to ask him. Why did he just leave us? Why hasn't he tried contacting us all these years? I'm worried one day it'll be too late."

She takes the papers from me and looks through them.

After a few minutes, she says, "What if he doesn't want to have anything to do with us?"

I swallow away the tears forming in my eyes. "Then at least we won't wonder anymore."

Henny lifts her head from the papers, her eyes circling over my face. "You've definitely matured these past few weeks, Adina. I don't think I'd be brave enough to face him at your age. Or even at my age. I wouldn't face it at all if you didn't bring this over."

"So you want to go?" I ask.

She looks back at the papers and sighs. "I do. Though it terrifies me."

"Me, too." I slip my hand into hers. She clutches mine tightly.

After a while she says, "We need to know why he left us. Even if he doesn't want to have anything to do with us, we still deserve an answer."

I nod, my heart hammering in my chest.

"Maybe we can see him later today," she says, rubbing her forehead again. "In the evening, when he'll be home."

"Okay." I squeeze her hand. Then I put the papers back in the envelope and stash it in my bag.

That Special Someone

Henny and I just sit on the couch, each buried in our thoughts. I wring my hands in my lap. She looks at me. "You seem sad. Not because of Dad. Something else."

Because of the moment we just shared together, I feel closer to her than I've felt in years. I lay my head on her shoulder and tell her everything that happened with Josh. When I'm done, my face is soaked with tears and I'm in Henny's arms. She's rubbing my back.

"I don't know why you're having such a hard time," she says, continuing to rub my back. "You're such a good person. You'll be a wonderful wife and mother one day." She pulls out of the hug and looks into my eyes. "Do you want to marry him?"

"What?"

"Yehoshua Markus. Do you want to marry him?"

I run my sleeve across my eyes. "I do. I've never felt this way about anyone before. I really thought he was the one for me."

"Adina, if you want him, go get him."

I just stare at her. Is my sister telling me to *chase* after a guy?

"Don't let him slip away from you," she says. "If there's one thing Dad leaving taught me, it's that you need to go after the things you want. Maybe if we wouldn't have just sat back and accepted it, maybe Dad would still be in our life. If Yehoshua Markus is the guy you want, don't let him slip away. Go after him, and don't give up until he tells you yes."

The tears slide down my cheeks. "But what if he doesn't want me? I don't want to get rejected again. I wouldn't bear it."

"But will you be able to bear wondering about him for the rest of your life? It's obvious he cares a lot about you. He went through all the trouble to hire an investigator to find out information about Dad. I've seen you struggle to find the right guy all these years. Now that you found him, you can't let him get away."

More tears splat down my cheeks as her words spin around in my head. She's right. Josh is the right guy for me. I *know* he is. I'll chase him down and won't give up on him. On us.

Chapter Twenty-Six

Henny and I hold hands as we approach my father's apartment.

We almost backed out at the last minute because we're both so nervous. What if he throws us out? What if he tells us he left us because we were a disappointment to him?

I tell myself to relax. Whatever happens at this meeting will be for the best. If my father wants to have a relationship with me, I'll be ecstatic. If he doesn't, I'll just move on with my life.

Henny and I make a short stop a few feet away from the door. She looks at me and I look at her. We both take a deep breath. Giving her an encouraging nod, I step forward and look at the name near the bell. Ephraim Reid. This is the last chance to back out. But I won't.

I ring the bell, then I return to my spot near Henny and

take her hand. She squeezes mine.

There's no answer. Maybe he's not home.

I'm about to ring the bell again when the door springs open. The man from the photo, the man who's been buried in my memories, stands before me. His brown eyes move from Henny to me, from me to Henny. He stumbles back, his eyes filled with nothing but pure shock.

He stares at us for what feels like forever. Henny and I stand still.

"Henny," he breathes. "Dini." He makes a move like he wants to wrap us in his arms, but he steps back. But then he seems to change his mind because he sprints forward and envelops us in his arms. "My girls." He kisses Henny's cheek, then mine. "My girls are here."

I know I should yank out of his hold. I should tell him he has no right to touch me, not after what he did to me fifteen years ago. But his embrace is so familiar, so comforting. I've missed it, so so much.

It appears as though he missed it just as much, because he doesn't let go.

Finally, we pull apart. He has tears in his eyes. So do I, and Henny, too. "Please come in," he says gesturing into the apartment.

My sister and I walk inside. It looks like a really small apartment, with a small kitchen, a sitting area, and what I imagine is one bedroom and a bathroom further down. Dad's hands shake as he motions toward the couch. "Please sit. Can I get you anything? A drink?"

"I'm okay, thanks," Henny says.

"Me, too."

Dad nods. Henny and I sit on the couch and he takes the chair across from us. The only sound I hear is the ticking of the clock.

"I'm so happy you're here," he says, fresh tears gathering in his eyes. "You have no idea how long I've dreamed of this."

Henny doesn't say anything. Neither do I. I don't know what to say. I have so many things to ask, but I'm afraid. He seems so kind, so hospitable. Like the dad I grew up with. Why in the world did he leave us?

Dad locks his hands together. "How did you find me?"

"A friend of mine tracked you down," I say. "Did you...did you not want to be found?"

He shakes his head, sighing. "It's a long story."

Henny says, "We have time. Actually, we had fifteen years."

Dad winces. "You're right. You're absolutely right." His lower lip trembles. "I didn't want to leave you girls. But I had no choice. I had to protect you."

Protect us? From what?

"I did business with a man," he says. "I found out that what he was doing was illegal. And not just illegal—he owed money to many people. A lot of shady people. I was so scared he'd come after me and my family, so I ran away. I transferred all the money I had into the bank account I shared with your mother so I knew she would be okay for the first few months." His gaze drops to his knees. "I loved you so much. Each and every one of you. But the only way to keep you safe was to run away."

I just sit still as I process what he's telling me. Henny does the same.

"Eventually, the cops found me innocent and I testified against my business partner and the other men in court. I was so worried their family members would come after me. That's the reason I never made contact with you. I thought keeping my distance would keep you safe."

"It's been fifteen years," Henny says. "A long time."

A hard swallow makes its way down his throat. "I thought

you'd never want to see me again. I thought it would be better if I was dead to you." He slowly and hesitantly lifts his eyes to us. "That doesn't mean I didn't stop caring. I heard your mother made a great life for you, that most of you got married and have built wonderful lives for yourselves. I didn't think you'd want me to come and disrupt everything."

Ever since my dad left, I told myself he had a valid reason for leaving, that he didn't just abandon us. And now I'm learning that he did have a good reason—he was trying to protect us.

When I glance at Henny, I still see distrust in her eyes. I know my father. I know he's a good man. I get up and bend forward to give him a hug. He seems caught off guard because he just sits still before returning it. After a bit, Henny gets up, too, and puts her arms over us.

"My girls," Dad says. "I'm sorry for everything that happened. I just needed to keep you safe."

"I understand," I tell him. "I knew deep down that you had to have a good reason for leaving us."

"My Dini." He flicks my nose like he always did when I was a kid. He then does it to Henny, which produces a small laugh out of her.

"I want to be part of your lives," he says. "I've wanted to for so many years. Can you forgive me and welcome me back in?"

I look at Henny. She looks at me. "It'll take some time," she says. "But I do want you back in my life. I want my children to get to know their grandfather."

"I want you in my life, too," I say. "And I think Mom and our brothers would want you, too."

He puts his arms around us again. "You have no idea how happy I am to hear this."

Chapter Twenty-Seven

Mr. Markus seems surprised to see me walk into his office the next day. "Yes, Adina?"

"I'd like to know where Yehoshua is staying."

He sighs. "Adina, I already told you—"

"You've seen your son struggling to find the right woman. Tell me right here and now that he's never been happier than when he was with me."

Mr. Markus sighs again. "Yes, he's been much happier since he met you. That's the reason I told him to reconsider leaving. But I couldn't get through to him. I don't want you to get hurt. If Yehoshua wants to speak to you, he'll seek you out."

I shake my head. "I'm not going to sit back and wait for him. I want to talk to him. He needs to understand that he can't just give up on us. Please, Mr. Markus. I really need to talk to him."

He hesitates.

"Don't worry about me getting hurt. I need to know if your son and I have a chance. I *need* to."

He's quiet for a little bit before he reaches for the pad of paper on his desk. He writes something down and hands it to me. It's an address in New Jersey.

"He's staying with his aunt," he tells me.

"Thanks," I say. "I'm taking the day off."

I call Mom and ask her if I can pick the car up from the hospital. I tell her I want to drive to New Jersey to speak to Josh. She tries to advise me not to make such a long trip when the boy might reject me again, but I tell her I'm okay and that I need to do this. She assures me I can take the car and she'll catch a ride home with one of her coworkers.

She meets me outside to give me the key and wraps her arms around me. "Be careful." She kisses my cheek.

"I'll be okay."

I get in the car and drive to New Jersey. On the way, I try to rehearse what I'll say to him, but I stop because I don't want to have a prepared speech. I want to talk from my heart.

Oddly, the ride takes shorter than I expect. I find the house and park in the driveway. I sit in the car for a few minutes, making a short prayer, asking God to guide me through this, to put the right words in my mouth.

When my heart is beating at a somewhat steady pace, I get out of the car and walk up to the house. My knees are knocking into each other and I almost trip as I climb up the stairs. Telling myself to calm down, I raise my hand and ring the bell.

The door opens to reveal a middle-aged woman. "Can I help you?"

"Is Yehoshua Markus here?"

"One minute, please." She leaves the door slightly ajar, and then I hear her call, "Josh! Someone's here to see you."

The contents in my stomach are sloshing around. I'm going to throw up.

I hear footsteps, and then the door opens again. Josh stands before me. His eyes widen. "Dini?"

"Hi, Josh."

"What are you doing here?"

"I need to talk to you."

He runs a trembling hand through his hair. "I…I…"

"Please, just hear me out."

He nods. "We'll have privacy in the backyard."

Walking side by side is so familiar, so comforting. I wonder if he feels the same. He stops before a swing set and sits on one of the swings. I sit on the other one.

Quiet.

The cool breeze blows against my face. It feels soothing.

More silence. Josh sways a little on his swing.

"You left," I say.

He nods.

"You didn't return my calls or texts."

He nods again.

Silence.

"Say something," I say. "Please."

He shakes his head, his eyes on his shoes. "I mess everything up."

"What are you talking about?"

"My parents are in debt because of me. Because of me, a girl had to leave a job she loved. I ruined her life. I don't want to ruin yours."

"You didn't ruin Suri's life, Josh. You have to stop beating yourself up over it. It's something that just happened. And you made a mistake by trusting the wrong guy and he cost you and your parents lots of money. You need to forgive yourself."

That Special Someone

His gaze is still locked on his shoes. "I went behind your back and hired an investigator to track down your father. I betrayed your trust. I hurt you. I don't think I can ever forgive myself for that. You're the greatest thing to happen to me. I messed it all up. I ruined everything."

"That's where you're wrong."

His head snaps up to mine. "What?"

"It's because of you that I met my father. If not for you, I wouldn't have made peace with him. Because of you, he will once again be part of my family's life."

He seems to be at a loss of words. Then, "You met your dad?"

I nod. "I visited him with my sister yesterday. He told me why he left us."

"Dini, that's amazing. I'm so happy for you."

"I couldn't have done it without you. Don't you see, Josh? You're not ruining my life, you're making it better. Out of all the guys I've dated—and believe me, there were many—none of them have made me feel the way you do. None of them have accepted me for who I am. I have so much more confidence now. It's all because of you."

He has tears in his eyes. "I love you, Dini," he whispers. "I think I have since the first moment I saw you. Though I don't know if I can say that." He laughs lightly. "But I hurt you. I lost your trust."

"Being in a relationship means you have to keep working on it. Yes you hurt me, but I hurt you, too. All couples go through rough patches. But if they can apologize and forgive one another and communicate, they can have a great, lasting relationship. I want that with you. I want to have a future with you."

"I want that, too."

"I don't want you to run away when things get tough. We have to stop being afraid to open our hearts. I want to be there for you, in every part of your life. I want to support your music. I want to hear what's in your heart. I want to be your best friend."

"I want that, too, Dini. I want to support you in every part of your life, whether it be programming or anything else. You're right—I am afraid to open my heart. I'm afraid to get hurt. But it's okay to feel vulnerable sometimes, as long as we're honest with each other and can work through it."

I nod. "I love you, too Joshter the Lobster. I'm so lucky to have found my special someone."

That Special Someone

He gives me the warmest smile he's ever given me. "Dini the Shrimpi, I'm lucky to have met my special someone, too."

Hebrew/Yiddish Glossary:

- Baruch Hashem (Hebrew)—thank God
- Bentch/Bentching (Yiddish)—reciting grace after meals
- Chuppah (Hebrew)—wedding canopy
- Frum (Yiddish)—observant Jew
- Get (Hebrew)—Jewish divorce
- Hashem (Hebrew)—God
- Mazel Tov (Hebrew/Yiddish)—congratulations and good wishes
- Mechitza (Hebrew)—partition, separating men and women
- Nachas (Hebrew)—joy and pride
- Shabbos (Hebrew)—Sabbath
- Sheitel (Yiddish)—wig
- Shul (Yiddish)–synagogue
- Sheva brochos (Hebrew)—a week of celebration and blessings following a wedding
- Simcha (Hebrew)—happiness or a joyous occasion

such as an engagement, wedding or bar/bas mitzvah

- Talmud (Hebrew)—the oral laws of the Torah that were later written down. It's comprised of the Mishna and Gemara

- Yeshiva (Hebrew)—Jewish day school

About the Author

Chaya T. Hirsch is an Orthodox Jewish woman who lives in New York. She is the author of *Meant To Be*, *That Special Someone*, *Shira's Secret*, *Aviva's Pain*, *Malky's Heart*, and *Losing Leah*. She is currently working on her next novel.

For updates on future releases, you can follow the author on Facebook.

Made in the USA
Las Vegas, NV
20 September 2023

77882020R00194